A Library of Modern Religious Thought

JOHN LOCKE
The Reasonableness of Christianity

A LIBRARY OF
MODERN RELIGIOUS THOUGHT
General Editor: Henry Chadwick, D.D.

S. T. COLERIDGE
CONFESSIONS OF AN INQUIRING SPIRIT
Edited by H. StJ. Hart

LESSING'S THEOLOGICAL WRITINGS
Selected and translated by Henry Chadwick

DAVID HUME
THE NATURAL HISTORY OF RELIGION
Edited by H. E. Root

S. KIERKEGAARD
JOHANNES CLIMACUS and A SERMON
Translated and edited by T. H. Croxall

JOHN LOCKE
THE REASONABLENESS OF CHRISTIANITY
Edited and abridged by I. T. Ramsey

THE MIND OF
THE OXFORD MOVEMENT
Edited by Owen Chadwick

JOHN LOCKE

THE REASONABLENESS
OF CHRISTIANITY

with
A Discourse of Miracles and
part of *A Third Letter Concerning Toleration*

EDITED, ABRIDGED, AND INTRODUCED BY
I. T. RAMSEY
Nolloth Professor of the Philosophy of
the Christian Religion
in the University of Oxford

STANFORD UNIVERSITY PRESS
STANFORD, CALIFORNIA

Stanford University Press
Stanford, California
© 1958 by A. and C. Black Ltd.
Original American edition 1958
Printed in the United States of America
ISBN 0-8047-0341-8
Last figure below indicates year of this printing:
83 82 81 80 79 78 77 76 75 74

CONTENTS

PREFACE

Apart from a few errata which were corrected in the second edition, there have been only very minor variations in the text of *The Reasonableness of Christianity* since the first edition of 1695; and the same is true of *A Third Letter concerning Toleration* which was published in 1692; and of *A Discourse of Miracles*, which was written in 1702 and first published posthumously in 1706. For convenience, the text of *The Reasonableness of Christianity* is reprinted from the 1731 edition; for the other reprints the text of the sixth edition of Locke's works (1759) has been used.

The Reasonableness of Christianity is a long document, and here especially, as Leslie Stephen observed generally of Locke's controversies, "Locke has no mercy on the patience of his readers". So it seemed wise to abridge the text at various points. Such abridgments are mainly by way of giving fewer scriptural discussions here and there. Very occasionally repetition of points which Locke makes elsewhere in the printed text has been omitted.

So that the reader may see for himself the extent and character of this abridgment, and also to facilitate reference, the paragraphs in this edition are numbered for the first time. A gap in enumeration means a paragraph omitted; a bracket round the paragraph number means that only a part of the original paragraph has been retained. A plain number means that the whole of the original paragraph has been printed. I hope that in this way the edition will provide abridgment without deception, and readability with usefulness. Further, the text has been modernized when this seemed also likely to contribute to its readability, and Locke's biblical references have been given the occasional correction they needed.

The text of *A Discourse of Miracles* is printed in full.

I.T.R.

EDITOR'S INTRODUCTION

I. BIOGRAPHICAL NOTE

John Locke was born of a fairly well-to-do family at Wrington, a village in North Somerset not far from Bristol, on 29th August 1632. He was 16 when Charles I was beheaded; 27 at the Restoration; 56 when William of Orange became king. Most of his early years thus coincided with years of civil war, and throughout his life men were but rarely unmoved by controversies of faith and of public duty.

At the age of about 14 he was admitted to Westminster School, and something of his life there can be discerned in his *Thoughts Concerning Education* (1693) where he criticized most severely the discipline and studies of English schools. In 1652 he became a scholar of Christ Church, Oxford, and, later, a Tutor and Censor. His future concern with public affairs was somewhat foreshadowed when in 1665-6 he acted as secretary to Sir Walter Vane on a mission to the Elector of Brandenburg. Back in Oxford, he prepared for a medical career, and it was for medical reasons that Lord Ashley—afterwards First Earl of Shaftesbury—first saw him when on a visit to Oxford. This acquaintance blossomed into a friendship which helped Locke to form the acquaintance of many men of letters and science, and politicians. This was the setting in which those discussions took place whose outcome was eventually to be the *Essay Concerning Human Understanding*.

In 1672 Ashley became Lord High Chancellor, and Locke continued in his service, being tutor to both the Second and Third Earls of Shaftesbury. When in 1682 Shaftesbury began to plan with Monmouth, Russell and others for a rising against the king, the plot was soon discovered and Shaftesbury managed to escape to Holland. Though we have no evidence that Locke was concerned in the plot, enough suspicion surrounded him for it to be prudent for him to leave for Holland in 1683, and he remained there until after the Revolution of 1688. It was there that a time of leisure enabled him to complete his *Essay Concerning Human Understanding*, the *Epistula de Tolerantia* and other works.

He took a principal share in the negotiations which placed William of Orange on the throne of England, and returned ultimately to England in the company of Queen Mary. His health, which had never been good, had by this time become very enfeebled, and refusing at least one diplomatic post he took up residence in 1691 with Sir Francis and Lady Masham in their manor house of Oates in Essex. Lady Masham was the daughter of Dr. Ralph Cudworth, the Cambridge Platonist, and had been well known to Locke before his retirement to Holland. It was here that he wrote *The Reasonableness of Christianity*, and it was from here that he published his fourth and last edition of the *Essay*. Despite his health he was, first, a Commissioner of Appeals, and then he held an important post at the Board of Trade, and when eventually in 1700 he retired, a constant flow of visitors to Oates maintained his connection with the world of affairs.

Not only the *Essay*, but both the *Epistula de Tolerantia* and *The Reasonableness of Christianity* brought him into much controversy. *The Reasonableness of Christianity* in particular brought a charge of unitarianism against him. A certain Cambridge clergyman, John Edwards,[1] attacked Locke's views on revelation and the person of Jesus, thus adding his criticisms to those, for example, of Edward Stillingfleet, Bishop of Worcester, who had already judged that Locke's doctrine of substance in the *Essay* compromised the doctrine of the Trinity. While Locke never cared for controversial writing, he entered into discussion with force and candour, and though the criticisms brought by his opponents were perhaps more far-reaching than even they supposed, Locke at any rate was always of the mind that his writings did full justice to the Christian faith.

He died on 28th October 1704, and it is said that Lady Masham read psalms to him almost up to the moment of his death. He was a humble-minded man, kind, cheerful and good-natured, who after a full life of learning and affairs could think of himself as no more than an under-labourer, and his epitaph (written by himself) in the churchyard at High Laver significantly remarks: ". . . tantum profecit ut veritati unice litaret; hoc ex scriptes illius disce; quae quod de eo reliquum est, majori fide tibi exhibibunt quam epitaphii suspecta elogia", which has been translated: ". . . he advanced just so far as to make an acceptable offering to truth alone; this learn from his writings, which will display to you with a greater reliability than the doubtful eulogies of an epitaph, what remains to be said about him".

[1] See footnote, p. 18.

2. FAITH AND REASON

In "The Epistle to the Reader" which prefaces *An Essay Concerning Human Understanding* Locke tells us "that five or six friends meeting at my chamber, and discoursing on a subject very remote from this, found themselves quickly at a stand by the difficulties that rose on every side. After we had a while puzzled ourselves, without coming any nearer a resolution of those doubts which perplexed us, it came into my thoughts, that we took a wrong course; and that, before we set ourselves upon enquiries of that nature, it was necessary to examine our own abilities, and see what objects our understandings were or were not fitted to deal with."[1]

One of these friends, a certain James Tyrrell, in a manuscript note in his copy of the *Essay* (now in the British Museum) tells us that the friends were discussing "the principles of morality and revealed religion". We may think that so far as religion went the difficulty was that "hard or misapplied words, with little or no meaning, have, by prescription, such a right to be mistaken for deep learning and height of speculation, that it will not be easy to persuade either those who speak or those who hear them, that they are but the covers of ignorance, and hindrance of true knowledge".[2] Against such pretensions and hindrances Locke's aim was "to break in upon this sanctuary of vanity and ignorance" and more positively "to enquire into the origins, certainty, and extent of human knowledge".[3] What in particular could be reasonably believed about the Christian faith? How far and in what way could there be genuine knowledge about religion?

To see Locke's broadest answer to these questions we may pass at once to Bk. IV, Ch. 17, para. 23, of the *Essay* where Locke makes a distinction between "above, contrary, and according to reason". He explains this distinction as follows:

"(1) *According to reason* are such propositions whose truth we can discover by examining and tracing those ideas we have from sensation and reflection, and by natural deduction find to be true or probable.

(2) *Above reason* are such propositions whose truth or probability we cannot by reason derive from those principles.

[1] *An Essay concerning Human Understanding* ed. and abridged A.S. Pringle-Pattison, "The Epistle to the Reader", p. 4.   [2] Ibid, p. 7.
[3] *An Essay Concerning Human Understanding*, Bk. I, Ch. 1, para. 2.

(3) *Contrary to reason* are such propositions as are inconsistent with or irreconcilable to our clear and distinct ideas. Thus the existence of one God is according to reason; the existence of more than one God is contrary to reason; the resurrection of the dead above reason."

(1) and (3) need not detain us long. No religion would wish to deny truths which in Locke's sense are "according to reason". These are truths reached by the mind when it exercises itself about those idea particulars which Locke had taken in Book II, Chapter 1, to be at the basis of all knowledge. Between such ideas we discern intuitively agreements or disagreements—we see, for example, that yellow differs from white, heat from cold, soft from hard, bitter from sweet (to take Locke's own examples, Bk. II, Ch. 1, para. 3), and from such a starting point by "natural deduction", which moves with intuitive certainty between steps which are intuitively recognized as indubitable, we formulate reliable propositions. Nor would a religious man wish to assert propositions which were clean contrary to reason, which were utterly "inconsistent with or irreconcilable to our clear and distinct ideas". No religion, for instance, must ask us to believe that black is white or a triangle is a circle. Now, Locke believed that by natural deduction we could not avoid arriving at the proposition that God exists; "the existence of a God reason clearly makes known to us" (*Essay*, Bk. IV, Ch. 10, para. 1). To suppose, therefore, that there could be more than one God would be to suppose that the same deductive argument could lead to more than one conclusion. Here is the background to the examples which Locke gives above, and so far everything is reasonably clear.

The real puzzle and the greatest interest centres on the propositions which are "above reason", and these are propositions for which a deductive pattern linking them with idea particulars is not to be found. The assent to such propositions Locke tells us is faith, and he makes the following distinction between reason and faith:

"*Reason* therefore here, as contradistinguished to faith, I take to be the discovery of the certainty or probability of such propositions or truths, which the mind arrives at by deductions made from such ideas which it has got by the use of its natural faculties, viz., by sensation or reflection.

Faith, on the other side, is the assent to any proposition, not thus made out by the deductions of reason, but upon the credit of the proposer, as coming from God in some extraordinary way of communication. This way of discovering truths to men we call *revelation.*" (Bk. IV, Ch. 18, para. 2.)

At the same time Locke is anxious to insist that such faith must be regulated, so that even when we assent to any proposition by faith our assent is, in a wider sense of the word, reasonable. He has said a little earlier (Bk. IV, Ch. 17, para. 24) that "faith is nothing but a firm assent of the mind; which if it be regulated, as is our duty, cannot be afforded to anything but upon good reason".

In this wider sense of reason then, what reasons could we have for making the assent of faith? The case, let us remember, is of a proposition which has not been "made out by the deductions of reason", that is, a proposition for which no deductive pattern can be found linking it to certain ideas. The question now becomes, what reason have we for accepting "the credit of the proposer" who claims that a certain proposition like this has been adumbrated to him by revelation? Not that the question escapes Locke, for he raises it explicitly in Book IV, Chapter 19, para. 10, where he is discussing Enthusiasm—the habit of giving unreasonable assent to religious propositions. When we "examine a little soberly this internal light and this feeling" on which enthusiasts build so much, the question is: "How do I know that God is the revealer of this to me; that this impression is made upon my mind by his Holy Spirit and that therefore I ought to obey it?" Or again, Bk. IV, Ch. 19, para. 13, ". . . how shall anyone distinguish between the delusions of Satan and the inspirations of the Holy Ghost?"

In *An Essay Concerning Human Understanding* we are not given a very adequate answer to this question. Such comments as Locke gives us are contained in Chapter 18 to which we have already referred, and in Chapter 19.

He first mentions two negative criteria and a trivial positive one. No one can claim to be inspired by God, no one can ask for an assent of faith, if the proposition he utters is "contradictory to our clear intuitive knowledge" (Bk. IV, Ch. 18, para. 5). Nor can anyone enunciate any revealed propositions about "new simple ideas": "whatever things were discovered to St. Paul when he was rapt up into the third heaven; whatever new ideas his mind there received, all the description he can make to others of that place is only this, that there are such things as 'eye hath not seen, nor ear heard, nor hath it entered into the heart of man to conceive'." Even if anyone had a "sixth sense" he could not talk about it intelligibly. Thirdly, we must *understand* any propositions to which we are expected to give the assent of faith (Bk. IV, Ch. 16, para. 14, and Ch. 18, para. 7).

In these ways, as he concludes Book IV, Chapter 19, "reason must be our last judge and guide in everything". But we might legitimately feel that it does not take us very far. Can Locke say nothing more about propositions which are "above reason", and whose deductive links with idea particulars are not to be found?

He can, and makes his point at the end of Chapter 19 of Book IV. The deductive links are not required, because as in the case of "the holy men of old who had revelations from God" we are given, with the propositions, "outward signs to convince [us] of the Author of those revelations" (Bk. IV, Ch. 19, para. 15). This then, so far as *An Essay Concerning Human Understanding* goes, is Locke's answer to the question he set himself at the start. What reason have we for accepting "credit of the proposer" who asks us to give a faith assent to a particular proposition? Locke's answer will be that this reasonableness will turn on "outward signs". But are we, with these "outward signs", in fact back merely with sensible ideas? Has the deductive link between idea particulars and propositions been replaced by nothing in the case of revealed propositions? When, as we shall see, these "outward signs" are miracles and fulfilled prophecies, have we to suppose that Locke's treatment of those topics involves nothing more than idea particulars, with which are just associated *ad hoc* revealed propositions? These are the crucial questions.

It is to consider these questions that we must turn from the sketch which Locke gives us of his views on revelation in *An Essay Concerning Human Understanding* to the more detailed exposition which we find in *The Reasonableness of Christianity as delivered in the Scriptures*, as well as in *A Discourse of Miracles*.

In *The Reasonableness of Christianity* the outline background of his views on revelation, which Locke has given us in the *Essay*, is filled out by particular reference to the Christian faith. In this case the proposer is Jesus of Nazareth, and the revealed truths which the Christians are to believe are those propositions to which the assent of faith is asked on the credit of the proposer as coming from God. In short, says Locke, we are to believe the revealed truths of the Christian faith on the credit of Jesus of Nazareth, and the outward signs which make such belief reasonable are two: (1) fulfilment of the prophecies about the Messiah, and (2) the performance of miracles. Let us consider each briefly in turn.

(1) For Locke, the fulfilment of prophecy was the success of a prediction. For centuries before the Christian dispensation people had talked of a "Messiah", a word which Locke takes to be synonymous with the other titles used of Jesus, e.g. "Son of God". When at last Jesus of Nazareth appeared, the label fitted. We can reasonably believe what Jesus taught, we can assent to his propositions "as coming from God in some extraordinary way of communication" because of this extraordinary empirical prediction which has come off. What, then (if anything) corresponds to the deductive pattern which, in the narrowest sense of reasonable, links a reasonable assertion with the ideas on which it is based? Is there simply a person to which a descriptive label, already current, at long last fits? Is that an adequate account of Locke's view? May not Locke rather have implied that in bringing alongside the person of Jesus the Messiah label, there strikes us an aptness and appropriateness of the kind which strikes us when, for example, we see at long last the island corresponding to the map we have pondered for years, or the last piece in the jigsaw which is just what we had been told to expect. In other words, though Locke never says so, is it not possible that even in thinking of the Messiah as a descriptive label which fitted Jesus, Locke was appealing to some kind of disclosure situation which linked ideas and revealed propositions? Was he appealing to something he called elsewhere "intuition"? For as we saw, it was in an intuitive disclosure that the agreements and disagreements of the idea-particulars were seen. May there not be an intuitive link between idea particulars and revealed propositions? May not intuition play the same part for propositions which are above reason as demonstration does in the case of propositions which are according to reason? In this case the broad reasonableness of Christian assent would lie in its intuitive character.

But whether or not we allow that interpretation of Locke, we have plainly to recognize that as the years have gone by, the concept of prophecy fulfilment has come to be seen to be far more complicated than Locke allowed. There is no question of a straight prediction which comes off. Not only are the various titles of Jesus not synonymous; they hardly belong to the same logical areas. Furthermore, the Christian, if Jesus of Nazareth is to be what the Christian believes him to be, has to hold that no one label or group of labels hitherto in circulation *exactly* fitted the person of Jesus. Otherwise there is nothing novel in the Christian revelation. But the result of all these complications could be that we begin to see more and more that the Christian revelation depends for its reasonableness on something like that intuition which Locke might possibly imply in his discussion of prophecy fulfilment. The only difference the years have brought is this: It must now be an intuition which arises when a number of different labels are seen to fit an object to which none of these alone are adequate, such as is the case when we become intuitively aware of a cone by seeing various projections of it, or of a mountain by seeing various single aspects of it. Our previous map and jig-saw examples are too simple.

(2) We may reach something like the same conclusion about the reasonableness of Christianity from Locke's discussion of miracles. Here were "outward signs" indeed, wonderful goings-on. Here (it might be thought) were credentials plain enough for everyone to see, and once we saw them, we reasonably believed whatever proposal their performer made. Miracles were rather like the credentials of an ambassador or the passport of a citizen. We believed what a person said because of the miracles he carried about with him. Here is the simplest interpretation of Locke's view. But as his *Discourse of Miracles*[1] makes clear, the position is hardly so simple. What if two people utter propositions claiming our faith assent, and both bring with them wonderful credentials? The situation may be like that of Moses and the Egyptians, both of whom (we are told) produced the most astonishing serpents. Locke comes closest to the simplest interpretation when at one point he seems to make reasonableness turn on the comparative wonder of the "outward signs". The bigger the miracle, the more reasonably do we assent to propositions which accompany it. So when the snakes of Moses devour the snakes of the Egyptians, we believe what Moses says rather than what the Egyptians would propose. Or, if

[1] See pages 78–87 below.

one man who feeds a hundred people on fifty loaves says something which conflicts with what a man who feeds five thousand on two loaves tells us, we had better believe the latter rather than the former.

But here is empiricism at its crudest. It is an empiricism which would set between the miraculous "ideas" and the revealed propositions no sort of substitute link for the deductive pattern which a thoroughly reasonable assent would demand. Could it in *any* sense be reasonable? It is not surprising that a religious man like Locke has traces of a more adequate interpretation, and one which takes us back to the same point we made in the case of prophecy fulfilment.

To reach this fuller interpretation it is convenient to go to Locke's *Third Letter on Toleration*.[1] There, as we shall see, Locke is most anxious to distinguish the compelling force of a miracle and the compelling force of civil power.

Now we may notice that the power of civil law is a power which can, with suitable complications, be adequately treated in terms of idea particulars: fines, prison, execution, and the rest. If the power of a miracle is something other than this, something for which civil power can be no substitute, the suggestion is that the power of a miracle, though associated with idea particulars, is something which is in some other way quite distinctive. The power of miracle is not measurable power, it is not power according to law. This means, I suggest, that a miracle must be given the same compelling power as belongs to an intuition, for this is all Locke has in his journeyman's bag besides idea particulars. Then Locke can justly say (as he does) that to distinguish between a pretended revelation and that which is truly divine "we need but open our eyes to see and be sure which came from [God]".[2]

It is certainly very important to read what he says about miracles in *A Third Letter Concerning Toleration* along with what he says about them in *A Discourse of Miracles*. Otherwise the *Discourse* may seem to be arguing for no more than a "subjective" interpretation of miracles and a very crude empirical interpretation at that. Whereas I suggest that Locke's concept of miracle always has in it a reference to the power of God, and that it is this compelling power, which makes a miracle situation to be intuitively given, and never adequately assessed in terms of idea particulars alone. Nor need we be surprised about this. For we may recall the difficulties Locke has in his *Essay Concerning Human*

[1] See pages 88–99 below. [2] See page 84 below.

Understanding precisely with this concept of power. He says in effect (Bk. II, Ch. 21, para. 4) that while we have plainly given to us the idea of a body at rest and the idea of a body thereafter at motion, we are never in the same sense given the idea of "active power". Power, in short, can hardly be satisfactorily treated in terms of idea particulars. We need not be surprised, then, since the concept of miracle implies an awareness of active power, that Locke's *Discourse* leaves certain major questions unsolved, such as whether miracles can be adequately assessed in terms of the ideas—the *miracula*—they contain. For the concept of power is one he never significantly contained within his epistemology of idea particulars. But all that he need have said, and this he could have said, was that in the case of miracles, Christianity appeals in the last resort to situations which, centring on some idea particulars of the "external world", are characterized by an active power of which we are intuitively aware as we are of our active power in certain circumstances. Belief in miracle, and belief in Jesus Christ, is then neither more nor less reasonable than a belief in a "powerful personality", and in the case of Jesus a personality uniquely powerful.

We may conclude by briefly summarizing the two views which it is possible to find in Locke's writings. The less complicated and more straightforward view involves only idea particulars and propositions. Sometimes these propositions arise from the mind exercising itself on the particulars intuitively and in a deductive fashion. They are then according to reason. When the exercise is inconsistent with any such deductive pattern, the propositions are contrary to reason. Revealed propositions which are above reason have, on this simpler view, no sort of epistemological link with idea particulars, but just happen to be given *ad hoc* along with idea particulars of a certain special sort, namely those which fulfil predictions or are extraordinary wonders.

On the other view, revealed propositions are those which are given with certain idea particulars when, though there be no deductive links between the idea particulars and the propositions, the propositions are nevertheless linked with the idea particulars in an intuitive situation not unlike that we know when we intuit our own active power. I suggest that it is only if we take this wider view that we can say that Locke preserves both the reasonableness as well as the mystery and the distinctiveness of the Christian faith. Reasonableness arises because it appeals to no ontological peculiarity of which we have no echoes elsewhere; mystery and distinctiveness arise because the power of the gospel, like all active power we know, is only in part tractable in terms of idea particulars.

Without doubt Locke had a very genuine desire to preserve mystery, a matter which is quite plain from his controversial exchanges. The only point at issue then seems to be: did Locke ever claim irreducible mysteries, i.e. mysteries which are not matters of temporary ignorance, mysteries which do not somehow and some day become tractable in terms of idea particulars? If we are right, the answer to this question will depend entirely on the answer we give to the question as to whether a power situation is ever wholly exhaustible in terms of ideas. This is the question which for Locke—and for anyone who is concerned to enquire into the possibility of an empirical approach to the Christian faith—is crucial.

But whatever is true about Locke, his successors had notoriously neither a desire to have a complex epistemology nor a wish to sponsor mystery. As is well known, the sequel to Locke was John Toland (1670–1722) whose *Christianity not Mysterious* (1696) attempted nothing beyond the compass of reason. Not only would he exclude what is contrary to reason, he excluded what is above reason as well. Likewise Matthew Tindal (1657–1733) in his *Christianity As Old as the Creation, or the Gospel, a Republication of the Religion of Nature* (1730), was so concerned with the similarity between the Christian faith and natural religion as to conclude that the only difference between them was the manner in which they were delivered. The propositions of one were conveyed to us deductively. The propositions of the other came to us *ad hoc* along with miracles and fulfilled prophecies, as though revealed truths were the "commercials" in a television programme of Christian wonders. The Christian dispensation provided a pleasant method of taking in philosophical results.

It is plain what must happen if we wish both to defend empirically the reasonableness of Christianity, yet not become deists like Toland and Tindal. We must think further about the "intuition" whereby, for example in a miracle situation, we become aware of the power of God which is the Gospel about God, remembering that a clue to its character is given to us in the intuitive awareness we have of our own activity. The Christian gospel is about a power of God; it is not in the first instance a set of propositions at all. Locke reminds us that

to be clear about the claims of the Christian faith we must first be
clear about what is revealed, about its empirical basis. It is in relation
to that basis that its claims to be reasonable, and reasonably mysterious,
will stand or fall; and it is in relation to that basis that we must plot
the essential articles of the Christian faith. He says to a certain Mr.
Bold[1] who with the "calmness of a Christian, the gravity of a divine,
the clearness of a man of parts, and the civility of a well-bred man" had
defended him against Mr. Edwards[2] that he hoped that *The Reasonableness of Christianity* would be of use "especially to those who thought
either that there was no need of revelation at all, or that the revelation
of our Saviour required the believing of such articles for salvation which
the settled notion, or their way of reasoning in some, and want of
understanding in others, made impossible to them". He thought that
many objections of the deists were "against Christianity misunder-
stood", and he intended that his work should clarify the claims of

[1] This was Samuel Bold (1649–1737) who was a Rector of Steeple in the Isle of
Purbeck from 1682 to the end of his life—some fifty-five years. He was a notable
controversialist and in 1697 began a series of tracts supporting Locke's *Essay
Concerning Human Understanding* and *The Reasonableness of Christianity* against
attacks by the Rev. John Edwards who is mentioned in the footnote below. Bold
called the *Essay* "one of the best books that has been published for at least 1600
years". Edwards retorted by calling Bold "Mr. Locke's journeyman", a phrase
which was no doubt the contemporary equivalent of "fellow traveller". The
quotations in the text above are taken from Locke's *Second Vindication of the
Reasonableness of Christianity* where Locke explicitly acknowledged Bold's
support, and in 1703 Bold visited Locke at Oates. There Locke dissuaded him from
taking the controversy further, but after Locke's death he did, in fact, publish
controversial papers he had previously prepared on the subject.
[2] This was John Edwards, a Calvinistic Divine (1637–1716), some-time Fellow
of St. John's College, Cambridge, who later held various livings, most of them
in the town of Cambridge itself. Hardly had *The Reasonableness of Christianity*
been published before it was attacked as Socinian by Edwards in a pamphlet
entitled (1695) *Some Thoughts Concerning the Several Causes and Occasions of
Atheism, especially in the Present Age, with some Brief Reflections on Socinianism and
on a late book entitled: "The Reasonableness of Christianity as delivered in the
Scriptures"*. Locke replied with (1695) *A Vindication of the Reasonableness of
Christianity*, to which Edwards answered in 1696 with his *Socinianism Unmasked*.
It was at this point, in 1697, that Bold entered the field as well, and Locke published
a *Second Vindication of the Reasonableness of Christianity* in 1697. Except for Bold's
later interventions, Edwards had the last word of this stage of the controversy
when in 1698 he published *A Free but Modest Censure on the late Controversial
Writings and Debates of Mr. Edwards and Mr. Locke*.
  The Reasonableness of Christianity was translated into Dutch in 1729, into
German in 1733 and into French in 1740.

the Christian faith, and make more evident the reasonableness of its essential doctrines. Whether or not we applaud his prescribed cure, we may share his intentions and hopes.

3. THE CONTEMPORARY SIGNIFICANCE OF "THE REASONABLENESS OF CHRISTIANITY"

For many years it has been unfashionable to talk of the reasonableness of Christianity. Why? As we look back, the first place we stop for an answer is, without doubt, Hegel, who argued for the reasonableness of Christianity only at the cost of subordinating the Christian faith to his own philosophical scheme. Hegel defended the reasonableness of Christianity only by making the Christian faith a brand of popular metaphysics, whose claims and insights, in so far as they could be justified, were (he thought) fully preserved and more reliably expressed in his absolute idealism. But to many Christians it did not seem as if Hegel's idealism preserved the gospel intact, and if Hegel had to be the measure of reasonableness the inevitable conclusion was that the Christian faith must be unreasonable and proud of it.

The same difficulty had been anticipated a century before. Looking back to Locke, with what justification we must leave the reader to decide, the Deists, of whom Toland and Tindal are the best-known representatives, had argued for the reasonableness of Christianity only by taking away altogether its distinctiveness. The Christian faith was credible only where it was reasonable, and it was reasonable only where it repeated those beliefs and moral maxims which could be reached by anyone if they had the ability and time to work out independently a philosophical viewpoint. Once again the reasonableness of Christianity was defended only at the cost of diluting beyond recognition the Christian religion.

So the question properly arises: Can the Christian faith be claimed as both distinctive and reasonable? The examples of Toland, Tindal and Hegel might suggest only a negative answer. And yet if only a negative answer can be given, we must give up all idea of integrating the Christian faith with philosophical speculation and culture whether humanist or scientific. The Christian faith will preserve its distinctiveness only at the cost of being utterly irrelevant. Can then the liberal hopes of the Deists and Hegel be preserved while doing justice to the distinctiveness of the Christian faith, without which they are barren indeed?

Now it is well known that from the side of philosophy itself Hegel has in recent days come in for some severe criticism. Metaphysics has by no means the prestige it once had. But when an empirical turn of mind characterizes much contemporary philosophy, can we not hope for a better account of the Christian faith than Toland or Tindal would give us? It is in this setting that Locke can be profitable for contemporary study. Could he, and does he, as an empiricist, give a better account of the Christian faith than successors such as Toland or Tindal? Can we find in Locke, as the founder of eighteenth-century empiricism, some hints as to where the narrower empiricism of some of his successors is inadequate, and where also a broader empiricism might do more justice to the reasonableness and distinctiveness of the Christian faith than was ever possible when metaphysics of the old brand held sway? Here is the timeliness of Locke for our own day.

THE REASONABLENESS OF CHRISTIANITY

62. Other reasons which hindered Jesus from professing himself in express direct words to be the Messiah.

75. The whole pattern of Christ's teaching was such as to give opportunity for the Scriptures to be fulfilled, and for this reason he never declared himself openly to be the Messiah (78).

139. The choice of the Apostles and the last scenes of Our Lord's life are all appropriate to the whole pattern of his preaching. His Messiahship is never plainly stated until his life has amply fulfilled scriptural prophecies.

IV. *Faith and Works*

164. Is the belief that Jesus of Nazareth is the Messiah only a historical and not a justifying or saving faith?

166. What of the devils who believe Jesus to be the Messiah? Repentance is needed as well.

172. Further, belief in Jesus as the Messiah needs to be integrated not only with repentance but with a good life. Faith does not supplant the law but must be accompanied by appropriate action.

185. To this point in the book the author has set out what the Christian requires *to believe*. From this point he will set out what the Christian requires *to do*, and he does this by once again looking at the commands of Our Lord himself.

187. The Christian needs to show repentance; to keep all the moral precepts of the Old Testament, but besides this "Our Saviour's teaching" tells of the necessity for many works of charity, and in particular for a moral life to be determined with respect to a Last Judgment.

V. *Some Difficulties*

228. (a) What of those who lived before Jesus? Even they could show an appropriate faith as did the heroes of the Old Testament, e.g. Abraham.

230. (b) What of those who have never heard of the Gospel and who had not even the advantage of the Jews? Even they have an inner light, and by this inner light they will be judged.

VI. *What advantage then by Jesus Christ?*

234. The first and general answer is that this is a matter which we must leave to the wisdom of God. We ourselves have only "short

views and narrow understandings", and must not "take too much upon us".

At the same time there are a number of particular considerations which can be offered:

238. (1) Despite the fact that God can be discerned in nature, the world had made little use of reason to find him there. Sins, lust, carelessness and fear had the effect of leaving all theology to the priests, who themselves excluded reason so as to secure their empire on superstition. Since Christ, belief in one God has prevailed and spread itself. Nor was the Old Testament revelation sufficient, because, for example, the works of Moses were done in a corner, whereas the miracles of Jesus are plain for all to see.

241. (2) The unassisted reason finds it too hard "to establish morality in all its parts", so the clear commands of a Saviour king provide a surer way to morality.

244. (3) Jesus encouraged a spiritual worship which did away with "a numerous huddle of pompous, fantastical, cumbersome ceremonies".

245. (4) Further, the whole perception of rewards and punishments encourages people the more to a virtuous and pious life. Without rewards and punishments virtue by itself would have few followers.

246. (5) By Jesus Christ comes a promise of assistance for "the frailty of our minds and weakness of our constitutions".

VII. *Why were the Epistles written?*

247. The Epistles have their special points to make appropriate to their several occasions, but they do not add to the one fundamental article of faith, which is belief in Jesus as the Messiah.

VIII. *Concluding Reflections*

252. The reasonableness of the Christian dispensation: God has dealt with man as a patient and tender father. He gave him reason, and with it a law, but because of the frailty of man, sent the Saviour-King who by his commands, declarations and miracles should win the allegiance of "the bulk of mankind". So the Christian religion does not depend on "speculations and niceties, obscure terms and abstract notions", but demands belief in Jesus, whose credentials are the way he fulfilled prophecies and performed miracles.

THE PREFACE

The little satisfaction and consistency that is to be found in most of the systems of divinity I have met with, made me betake myself to the sole reading of the Scripture (to which they all appeal) for the understanding the Christian religion. What from thence, by an attentive and unbiassed search, I have received, reader, I here deliver to thee. If by this my labour thou receivest any light, or confirmation in the truth, join with me in thanks to the Father of lights, for his condescension to our understandings. If, upon a fair and unprejudiced examination, thou findest I have mistaken the sense and tenor of the gospel, I beseech thee, as a true Christian, in the spirit of the gospel (which is that of charity) and in the words of sobriety, set me right, in the doctrine of salvation.

THE REASONABLENESS OF CHRISTIANITY,
AS DELIVERED IN THE SCRIPTURES

1. It is obvious to any one, who reads the New Testament, that the doctrine of redemption, and consequently of the gospel, is founded upon the supposition of Adam's fall. To understand therefore what we are restored to by Jesus Christ, we must consider what the scripture shews we lost by Adam. This I thought worthy of a diligent and un-biassed search: since I found the two extremes, that men run into on this point, either on the one hand shook the foundations of all religion, or on the other made Christianity almost nothing. For whilst some men would have all Adam's posterity doomed to eternal infinite punish-ment, for the transgression of Adam, whom millions had never heard of, and no one had authorized to transact for him, or be his representa-tive; this seemed to others so little consistent with the justice or goodness of the great and infinite God, that they thought there was no redemption necessary, and consequently that there was none, rather than admit of it upon a supposition so derogatory to the honour and attributes of that infinite being; and so made Jesus Christ nothing but the restorer and preacher of pure natural religion; thereby doing violence to the whole tenor of the New Testament. And, indeed, both sides will be suspected to have trespassed this way, against the written Word of God, by any one, who does but take it to be a collection of writings, designed by God, for the instruction of the illiterate bulk of mankind, in the way to salvation; and therefore, generally, and in necessary points, to be understood in the plain direct meaning of the words and phrases, such as they may be supposed to have had in the mouths of the speakers, who used them according to the language of that time and country wherein they lived; without such learned, artificial, and forced senses of them, as are sought out, and put upon them, in most of the systems of divinity, according to the notions that each one has been bred up in.

2. To one that, thus unbiassed, reads the Scriptures, what Adam fell from, is visible, was the state of perfect obedience, which is called justice in the New Testament, though the word, which in the original

signifies justice, be translated righteousness: and, by this fall, he lost paradise, wherein was tranquillity and the tree of life, i.e. he lost bliss and immortality. The penalty annexed to the breach of the law, with the sentence pronounced by God upon it, shews this. The penalty stands thus, Gen. ii. 17, "In the day that thou eatest thereof thou shalt surely die." How was this executed? He did eat, but in the day he did eat, he did not actually die, but was turned out of paradise from the tree of life, and shut out for ever from it, "lest he should take thereof and live for ever". This shews that the state of paradise was a state of immortality, of life without end, which he lost that very day that he eat: his life began from thence to shorten and waste, and to have an end; and from thence to his actual death, was but like the time of a prisoner between the sentence passed and the execution, which was in view and certain. Death then entered, and shewed his face, which before was shut out, and not known, so St. Paul, Rom. v. 12, "By one man sin entered into the world, and death by sin"; i.e. a state of death and mortality: and, 1 Cor. xv. 22, "In Adam all die"; i.e. by reason of his transgression, all men are mortal, and come to die.

3. This is so clear in these cited places, and so much the current of the New Testament, that nobody can deny, but that the doctrine of the gospel is, that death came on all men by Adam's sin; only they differ about the signification of the word death: for some will have it to be a state of guilt, wherein not only he, but all his posterity was so involved, that every one descended of him deserved endless torment, in hell-fire. I shall say nothing more here, how far, in the apprehensions of men, this consists with the justice and goodness of God, having mentioned it above: but it seems a strange way of understanding a law, which requires the plainest and directest words, that by death should be meant eternal life in misery. Could any one be supposed, by a law, that says, "For felony thou shalt die", not that he should lose his life, but kept alive in perpetual exquisite torments? And would any one think himself fairly dealt with, that was so used?

4. To this, they would have it be also a state of necessary sinning, and provoking God, in every action that men do: a yet harder sense of the word death than the other. God says, "That in the day that thou eatest of the forbidden fruit, thou shalt die"; i.e. thou and thy posterity shall be ever after uncapable of doing any thing, but what shall be sinful and provoking to me, and shall justly deserve my wrath and

indignation. Could a worthy man be supposed to put such terms upon the obedience of his subjects? much less can the Righteous God be supposed, as a punishment of one sin wherewith he is displeased, to put a man under a necessity of sinning continually, and so multiplying the provocation? The reason of this strange interpretation we shall perhaps find in some mistaken places of the New Testament. I must confess by death here, I can understand nothing but a ceasing to be, the losing of all actions of life and sense. Such a death came on Adam, and all his posterity by his first disobedience in paradise, under which death they should have lain for ever, had it not been for the redemption by Jesus Christ. If by death threatened to Adam, were meant the corruption of human nature in his posterity, 'tis strange that the New Testament should not any where take notice of it, and tell us, that corruption seized on all because of Adam's transgression, as well as it tells us so of death. But, as I remember, every one's sin is charged upon himself only.

(6) As Adam was turned out of paradise, so all his posterity were born out of it, out of the reach of the tree of life; all, like their father Adam, in a state of mortality, void of the tranquillity and bliss of paradise. Rom. v. 12, "By one man sin entered into the world, and death by sin". But here will occur the common objection, that so many stumble at: "How doth it consist with the justness and goodness of God, that the posterity of Adam should suffer for his sin; the innocent be punished for the guilty?" Very well, if keeping one from what he has no right to be called a punishment; the state of immortality, in paradise, is not due to the posterity of Adam, more than to any other creature. Nay, if God afford them a temporary, mortal life, 'tis his gift they owe it to his bounty, they could not claim it as their right, nor does he injure them when he takes it from them. Had he taken from mankind any thing that was their right, or did he put men in a state of misery, worse than not being, without any fault, or demerit of their own; this, indeed, would be hard to reconcile with the notion we have of justice; and much more with the goodness, and other attributes of the supreme Being, which he has declared of himself, and reason, as well as revelation, must acknowledge to be in him; unless we will confound good and evil, God and Satan. That such a state of extreme, irremediable torment is worse than no being at all; if every one's own sense did not determine against the vain philosophy, and foolish

metaphysics of some men; yet our Saviour's peremptory decision, Matt. xxvi. 24, has put it past doubt, that one may be in such an estate, that it may be better for him not to have been born. But that such a temporary life, as we now have, with all its frailties and miseries, is better than no being, is evident, by the high value we put upon it ourselves. And therefore, though all die in Adam, yet none are truly punished, but for their own deeds.

7. Adam being thus turned out of paradise, and all his posterity born out of it, the consequence of it was, that all men should die, and remain under death for ever, and so be utterly lost.

8. From this estate of death, Jesus Christ restores all mankind to life; I Cor. xv. 22, "As in Adam all die, so in Christ shall all be made alive". How this shall be, the same Apostle tells us in the foregoing ver. 21, "By man death came, by man also came the resurrection from the dead." Whereby it appears, that the Life, which Jesus Christ restores to all men, is that life, which they receive again at the Resurrection. Then they recovered from death, which otherwise all mankind should have continued under, lost for ever, as appears by St. Paul's arguing, I Cor. xv, concerning the resurrection.

(9) If any of the posterity of Adam were just, they shall not lose the reward of it, eternal life and bliss, by being his mortal issue: Christ will bring them all to life again; and then they shall be put every one upon his own trial, and receive judgment, as he is found to be righteous or not. And the righteous, as our Saviour says, Matt. xxv. 46, shall go into eternal life. Nor shall any one miss it, who has done what our Saviour directed the lawyer, who asked, Luke x. 25, What he should do to inherit eternal life? Do this, i.e. what is required by the law, and thou shalt live.

11. Here then we have the standing and fixed measures of life and death; immortality and bliss belong to the righteous; those who have lived in an exact conformity to the law of God, are out of the reach of death: but an exclusion from paradise, and loss of immortality, is the portion of sinners, of all those, who have in any way broke that law, and failed of a complete obedience to it, by the guilt of any one transgression. And thus mankind, by the law, are put upon the issues of life and death, as they are righteous or unrighteous, just or unjust; i.e. exact performers or transgressors of the law.

12. But yet, "all having sinned", Rom. iii, 23, "and come short of

the glory of God", i.e. the kingdom of God in heaven, which is often called his glory, both Jews and Gentiles, ver. 22, so that, by the deeds of the law, no one could be justified, ver. 20, it follows, that no one could then have eternal life and bliss.

15. This then being the case, that whoever is guilty of any sin, should certainly die and cease to be, the benefit of life, restored by Christ at the resurrection, would have been no great advantage (for as much as, here again, death must have seized upon all mankind, because all had sinned; for the wages of sin is everywhere death, as well after, as before the resurrection) if God had not found out a way to justify some, i.e. so many as obeyed another law, which God gave, which in the New Testament is called the law of faith, Rom. iii. 27, and is opposed to the law of works. And therefore, the punishment of those who would not follow him, was to lose their souls, i.e. their lives, Mark viii. 35–38, as is plain, considering the occasion it was spoke on.

16. The better to understand the law of faith, it will be convenient, in the first place, to consider the law of works. The law of works then, in short, is that law which requires perfect obedience, without any remission or abatement; so that by that law a man cannot be just, or justified, without an exact performance of every tittle. Such a perfect obedience, in the New Testament, is termed δικαιοσύνη, which we translate righteousness.

(18) Where this law of works was to be found, the New Testament tells us, viz. in the law delivered by Moses.

19. "But the law, given by Moses, being not given to all mankind, how are all men sinners, since, without a law, there is no transgression?" To this the Apostle, ver. 14[1], answers, "For when the Gentiles, which have not the law, do" (i.e. find it reasonable to do) "by nature the things contained in the law; these having not the law, are a law unto themselves: Which shew the work of the law written in their hearts, their consciences also bearing witness, and amongst one another their thoughts accusing or excusing." By which, and other places in the following chapter, 'tis plain, that under the law of works is comprehended also the law of nature, knowable by reason, as well as the law given by Moses. "For", says St. Paul, Rom. iii, 9, 23, "We have proved both Jews and Gentiles, that they are all under sin: For all have sinned and come short of the glory of God": which they could not do, without a law.

[1] Romans 2.

20. Nay, whatever God requires any where to be done, without making any allowance for faith, that is a part of the law of works: so that forbidding Adam to eat of the tree of knowledge, was part of the law of works. Only we must take notice here, that some of God's positive commands being for peculiar ends, and suited to particular circumstances of times, places, and persons, having a limited and only temporary obligation by virtue of God's positive injunction; such as was that part of Moses's law which concerned the outward worship or political constitution of the Jews, and is called the ceremonial and Judaical law, in contradistinction to the moral part of it; which being conformable to the eternal law of right, is of eternal obligation, and therefore remains in force still under the gospel; nor is abrogated by the law of faith, as St. Paul found some ready to infer, Rom. iii. 31. "Do we then make void the law, through faith? God forbid; yea, we establish the law."

21. Nor can it be otherwise: for, were there no law of works, there could be no law of faith. For there could be no need of faith, which should be counted to men for righteousness, if there were no law to be the rule and measure of righteousness, which men failed in their obedience to. Where there is no law, there is no sin; all are righteous equally, with or without faith.

(22) The rule, therefore, of right is the same, that ever it was; the obligation to observe it is, also, the same: the difference between the law of works, and the law of faith, is only this; that the law of works makes no allowance for failing on any occasion. Those that obey are righteous; those that in any part disobey, are unrighteous, and must not expect life, the reward of righteousness. But by the law of faith, faith is allowed to supply the defect of full obedience; and so the believers are admitted to life and immortality, as if they were righteous. Only here we must take notice, that when St. Paul says, that the gospel establishes the law, he means the moral part of the law of Moses; for that he could not mean the ceremonial, or political part of it, is evident, by what I quoted out of him just now, where he says, that the Gentiles do, by nature, the things contained in the law, their consciences bearing witness. For the Gentiles neither did, nor thought of, the Judaical and ceremonial institutions of Moses; 'twas only the moral part, their consciences were concerned in.

23. Thus then, as to the law, in short: the civil and ritual part of the

law, delivered by Moses, obliges not Christians, though, to the Jews, it were a part of the law of works; it being a part of the law of nature, that man ought to obey every positive law of God, whenever he shall please to make any such addition to the law of his nature. But the moral part of Moses's law, or the moral law (which is every where the same, the eternal rule of right), obliges Christians and all men every where, and is to all men the standing law of works. But Christian believers have the privilege to be under the law of faith too; which is that law whereby God justifies a man for believing, though by his works he be not just or righteous, i.e. though he came short of perfect obedience to the law of works. God alone does, or can justify or make just those who by their works are not so; which he doth by counting their faith for righteousness, i.e. for a complete performance of the law. Rom. iv. 3, "Abraham believed God, and it was counted unto him for righteousness." Ver. 5, "To him that believeth on him that justifieth the ungodly, his faith is counted for righteousness." Ver. 6, "Even as David also describeth the blessedness of the man unto whom God imputeth righteousness without works"; i.e. without a full measure of works, which is exact obedience. Ver. 7, "Saying, Blessed are they whose iniquities are forgiven, and whose sins are covered." Ver. 8, "Blessed is the man, to whom the Lord will not impute sin."

24. This faith, for which God justified Abraham, what was it? It was the believing God, when he engaged his promise in the covenant he made with him. This will be plain to any one who considers these places together, Gen. xv. 6, "He believed in the Lord", or "believed the Lord": for that the Hebrew phrase "believing in", signifies no more but believing, is plain from St. Paul's citation of this place, Rom. iv. 3, where he repeats it thus: "Abraham believed God", which he thus explains, ver. 18–22, "Who against hope, believed in hope, that he might become the father of many nations: according to that which was spoken, so shall thy seed be. And being not weak in faith, he considered not his own body now dead, when he was about an hundred years old, nor yet the deadness of Sarah's womb. He staggered not at the promise of God through unbelief; but was strong in faith, giving glory to God: And being fully persuaded, that what he had promised he was also able to perform. And therefore it was imputed to him for righteousness." By which it is clear, that the faith which God counted to Abraham for righteousness, was nothing but a firm belief of what

God declared to him, and a steadfast relying on him, for the accomplishment of what he had promised.

(25) The law of faith then, in short, is for every one to believe what God requires him to believe, as a condition of the covenant he makes with him; and not to doubt of the performance of his promises. This the apostle intimates in the close here, ver. 24, "But for us also, to whom it shall be imputed, if we believe on him that raised up Jesus our Lord from the dead." We must, therefore, examine and see what God requires us to believe now, under the revelation of the gospel; for the belief of one invisible, eternal, omnipotent God, maker of heaven and earth, etc., was required before, as well as now.

26. What we are now required to believe to obtain eternal life, is plainly set down in the gospel. St. John tells us, John iii. 36, "He that believeth on the Son, hath eternal life; and he that believeth not the Son, shall not see life." What this believing on him is, we are also told in the next chapter. "The woman saith unto him, I know that the Messiah cometh: when he is come, he will tell us all things. Jesus said unto her, I that speak unto thee am he. The woman then went into the city, and saith to the men, Come see a man that hath told me all things that ever I did. Is not this the Messiah? And many of the Samaritans believed on him; for the saying of the woman, who testified, he told me all that ever I did. So when the Samaritans were come unto him, many more believed because of his words, and said to the woman, We believe not any longer, because of thy saying; for we have heard ourselves, and we know, that this man is truly the Saviour of the world, the Messiah," John, iv. 25, 26, 28, 29, 39, 40, 41, 42.

27. By which place it is plain, that believing on the Son, is the believing that Jesus was the Messiah; giving credit to the miracles he did, and the profession he made of himself. For those who were said to BELIEVE ON HIM, for the saying of the woman, ver. 39, tell the woman, that they now believed not any longer, because of her saying; but that having heard him themselves, they knew, i.e. BELIEVED, past doubt, THAT HE WAS THE MESSIAH.

28. This was the great proposition that was then controverted, concerning Jesus of Nazareth, whether he was the Messiah or no? and the assent to that, was that which distinguished believers from unbelievers. When many of his disciples had forsaken him, upon his declaring that he was the Bread of Life which came down from heaven,

he said to the apostles, "Will ye also go away? Then Simon Peter answered him; Lord, to whom shall we go? Thou hast the words of eternal life: And we believe, and are sure thou art the Messiah, the Son of the living God", John vi. 69. This was the faith which distinguished them from apostates and unbelievers, and was sufficient to continue them in the rank of apostles: and it was upon the same proposition, "that Jesus was the Messiah, the Son of the living God", owned by St. Peter, that Our Saviour said, he would build his Church, Matt. xvi. 16–18.

(29) To convince men of this, he did his miracles: and their assent to, or not assenting to this, made them to be, or not to be of his Church; believers, or not believers.

30. Accordingly the great question among the Jews was, whether he were the Messiah or no? And the great point insisted on and promulgated in the gospel was, that he was the Messiah. The first glad tidings of his birth, brought to the shepherds by an angel, was in these words: "Fear not, for behold I bring you good tidings of great joy, which shall be to all people; for to you is born this day in the city of David a Saviour, who is the Messiah, the Lord", Luke ii. 11. Our Saviour discoursing with Martha about the means of attaining eternal life, saith to her, John xi. 26, "Whosoever believeth in me, shall never die. Believest thou this? She saith unto him, Yea, Lord, I believe that thou art the Messiah, the Son of God, which should come into the world." This answer of hers sheweth what it is to believe in Jesus Christ, so as to have eternal life, viz. to believe that he is the Messiah the Son of God, whose coming was foretold by the prophets. And thus Andrew and Philip express it: Andrew says to his brother Simon, "We have found the Messiah, which is, being interpreted, the Christ." Philip saith to Nathaniel, "We have found him of whom Moses in the law, and the Prophets did write, Jesus of Nazareth, the Son of Joseph", John i. 41, 45. According to what the evangelist says in this place, I have, for the clear understanding of the Scripture, all along, put Messiah for Christ: Christ being but the Greek name for the Hebrew Messiah, and both signifying, the anointed.

31. And that he was the Messiah, was the great truth he took pains to convince his disciples and apostles of; appearing to them after his resurrection: as may be seen, Luke xxiv, which we shall more particularly consider in another place. There we read what gospel

Our Saviour preached to his disciples and apostles; and that, as soon as he was risen from the dead, twice, the very day of his resurrection.

32. And, if we may gather what was to be believed by all nations, from what was preached unto them; we may certainly know what they were commanded, Matt. ult. to teach all nations, by what they actually did teach all nations. We may observe, that the preaching of the apostles every where in the Acts tended to this one point, to prove that Jesus was the Messiah. Indeed, now after his death, his resurrection was also commonly required to be believed as a necessary article, and sometimes solely insisted on: It being a mark and undoubted evidence of his being the Messiah, and necessary now to be believed by those who would receive him as the Messiah. For since the Messiah was to be a saviour and a king, and to give life and a kingdom to those who received him, as we shall see by-and-by, there could have been no pretence to have given him out for the Messiah, and to require men to believe him to be so, who thought him under the power of death, and corruption of the grave. And therefore those who believed him to be the Messiah, must believe that he was risen from the dead: And those who believed him to be risen from the dead, could not doubt of his being the Messiah. But of this more in another place.

33. Let us see, therefore, how the apostles preached Christ, and what they proposed to their hearers to believe. St. Peter at Jerusalem, Acts ii. by his first sermon, converted three thousand souls. What was his word, which as we are told, ver. 41, "they gladly received, and thereupon were baptised"? That may be seen from ver. 22 to ver. 36. In short this, which is the conclusion drawn from all that he had said, and which he presses on them as the thing they were to believe, viz. "Therefore let all the house of Israel know assuredly, that God hath made that same Jesus, whom ye have crucified, Lord and Messiah", ver. 36.

36. What was Stephen's speech to the council, Acts vii. but a reprehension to them, that they were the betrayers and murderers of the Just One? Which is the title by which he plainly designs the Messiah whose coming was fore-shewn by the prophets, vers. 51, 52. And that the Messiah was to be without sin (which is the import of the word just) was the opinion of the Jews, appears from John ix. 22 compared with ver. 24.

37. Acts viii. Philip carries the gospel to Samaria. "Then Philip went down to Samaria, and preached to them." What was it he preached? You have an account of it in this one word, "The Messiah," ver. 5. This being that alone which was required of them, to believe that Jesus was the Messiah, which, when they believed, they were baptized. "And when they believed Philip's preaching the gospel of the kingdom of God, and the name of Jesus the Messiah, they were baptized, both men and women", ver. 12.

(38) Philip being sent from thence, by a special call of the Spirit, to make an eminent convert, out of Isaiah preaches to him Jesus, ver. 35. And what it was he preached concerning Jesus, we may know, by the profession of faith the eunuch made, upon which he was admitted to baptism, ver. 37, "I believe that Jesus Christ is the Son of God": which is as much as to say, I believe that he, whom you call Jesus Christ, is really and truly the Messiah, that was promised. For, that believing him to be the Son of God, and to be the Messiah, was the same thing, may appear, by comparing John i. 45, with ver. 49, where Nathaniel owns Jesus to be the Messiah, in these terms: "Thou art the Son of God; thou art the king of Israel." So the Jews, Luke xxii. 70, asking Christ whether he were the Son of God, plainly demand of him, whether he were the Messiah?

39. Acts ix. St. Paul exercising the commission to preach the gospel, which he had received in a miraculous way, ver. 20, "Straitway preached Christ in the synagogues, that he is the Son of God"; i.e. that Jesus was the Messiah: for Christ, in this place, is evidently a proper name. And that this was it, which Paul preached, appears from ver. 22. "Saul increased the more in strength, and confounded the Jews, who dwelt in Damascus, proving that this is the very Christ", i.e. the Messiah.

(40) And when some of the sect of the Pharisees, who believed thought "it needful that the converted Gentiles should be circumcized, and keep the law of Moses", Acts xv, "Peter rose up and said to them, men and brethren, you know that a good while ago God made choice amongst us, that the Gentiles", viz. Cornelius, and those here converted with him, "by my mouth should hear the gospel, and believe. And God, who knoweth the hearts, bare them witness, giving them the Holy Ghost, even as he did unto us, and put no difference between us and them, purifying their hearts by faith", vers. 7–9. So that both Jews

and Gentiles, who believed Jesus to be the Messiah, received thereupon the seal of baptism; whereby they were owned to be his, and distinguished from unbelievers.

(55) The profession, which John the Baptist made, when sent to the Jews, John i. 20, was, that "he was not the Messiah"; but that Jesus was. This will appear to any one, who will compare vers. 26–34, with John iii. 27, 30. The Jews being very inquisitive to know, whether John were the Messiah; he positively denies it; but tells them, he was only his fore-runner; and that there stood one amongst them, who would follow him, whose shoe-latchet he was not worthy to untie. The next day, seeing Jesus, he says, he was the man; and that his own baptizing in water, was only that Jesus might be manifested to the world; and that he knew him not, till he saw the Holy Ghost descend upon him, he that sent him to baptize, having told him, that he on whom he should see the Spirit descend, and rest upon, he it was that should baptize with the Holy Ghost; and that therefore he witnessed, that "this was the Son of God", ver. 34, i.e. the Messiah; and Ch. iii. 26, etc., they came to John the Baptist, and tell him, that Jesus baptized, and that all men went to him. John answers, He has his authority from heaven; you know I never said, I was the Messiah, but that I was sent before him. He must increase, but I must decrease; for God hath sent him, and he speaks the words of God; and God hath given all things into the hands of his son, "And he that believes on the Son, hath eternal life"; the same doctrine, and nothing else, but what was preached by the apostles afterwards; as we have seen all through the Acts, e.g. that Jesus was the Messiah. And thus it was, that John bears witness of our Saviour, as Jesus himself says, John v. 33.

56. This also was the declaration that was given of him at his baptism, by a voice from heaven: "This is my beloved Son in whom I am well pleased", Matt. iii. 17, which was a declaration of him to be the Messiah; the Son of God being (as we have shewed) understood to signify the Messiah. To which we may add the first mention of him after his conception, in the words of the angel to Joseph; Matt. i. 21, "Thou shalt call his name Jesus", or Saviour; "for he shall save his people from their sins". It was a received doctrine in the Jewish nation, that at the coming of the Messiah all their sins should be forgiven them. These words, therefore, of the angel, we may look upon as a declaration, that Jesus was the Messiah; whereof these words,

"his people", are a further mark; which suppose him to have a people, and consequently to be a king.

57. After his baptism, Jesus himself enters upon his ministry. But before we examine what it was proposed to be believed, we must observe, that there is a threefold declaration of the Messiah:

(58) 1. By miracles. The spirit of prophecy had now for many ages forsaken the Jews: and, though their commonwealth were not quite dissolved, but that they lived under their own laws, yet they were under a foreign dominion, subject to the Romans. In this state, their account of the time being up, they were in expectation of the Messiah, and of deliverance by him in a kingdom he was to set up, according to their ancient prophecies of him: which gave them hopes of an extraordinary man yet to come from God, who, with an extraordinary and divine power, and miracles, should evidence his mission, and work their deliverance. And, of any such extraordinary person, who should have the power of doing miracles, they had no other expectation, but only of their Messiah. One great prophet and worker of miracles, and only one more, they expected, who was to be the Messiah. And therefore we see the people justified their believing in him, i.e. their believing him to be the Messiah, because of the miracles he did; John vii. 31, "And many of the people believed in him, and said, When the Messiah cometh, will he do more miracles, than this man hath done?"

(59) 2. Another way of declaring the coming of the Messiah, was by phrases and circumlocutions, that did signify or intimate his coming; though not in direct words pointing out the person. The most usual of these were, "The kingdom of God, and of heaven"; because it was that which was often spoken of the Messiah, in the Old Testament, in very plain words: and a kingdom was that, which the Jews most looked after, and wished for.

(61) 3. By plain and direct words, declaring the doctrine of the Messiah, speaking out that Jesus was he; as we see the apostles did, when they went about preaching the gospel, after Our Saviour's resurrection. This was the open clear way, and that which one would think the Messiah himself, when he came, should have taken; especially, if it were of that moment, that upon men's believing him to be the Messiah, depended the forgiveness of their sins. And yet we see, that our Saviour did not: but on the contrary, for the most part, made no other discovery of himself, at least in Judea, and at the beginning of his ministry, but in

the two former ways, which were more obscure; not declaring himself to be the Messiah, any otherwise than as it might be gathered from the miracles he did, and the conformity of his life and actions, with the prophecies of the Old Testament concerning him; and from some general discourses of the kingdom of the Messiah being come, under the name of the "kingdom of God, and of heaven".

(62) This concealment of himself will seem strange, in one who was come to bring light into the world, and was to suffer death for the testimony of the truth. This reservedness will be thought to look, as if he had a mind to conceal himself, and not to be known to the world for the Messiah, nor to be believed on as such. But we shall be of another mind, and conclude this proceeding of his according to divine wisdom, and suited to a fuller manifestation and evidence of his being the Messiah; when we consider, that he was to fill out the time foretold of his ministry; and, after a life illustrious in miracles and good works, attended with humility, meekness, patience, and sufferings, and every way conformable to the prophecies of him, should be led as a sheep to the slaughter, and with all quiet and submission be brought to the cross, though there were no guilt, nor fault found in him. This could not have been, if, as soon as he appeared in public, and began to preach, he had presently professed himself to have been the Messiah; the king that owned that kingdom, he published to be at hand. For the Sanhedrim would then have laid hold on it, to have got him into their power, and thereby have taken away his life; at least, they would have disturbed his ministry, and hindered the work he was about. That this made him cautious, and avoid, as much as he could, the occasions of provoking them, and falling into their hands, is plain from John vii. 1, "After these things Jesus walked in Galilee": out of the way of the chief priests and rulers; "for he would not walk in Jewry, because the Jews sought to kill him".

73. And here we may observe the wonderful providence of God, who had so ordered the state of the Jews, at the time when his son was to come into the world, that though neither the civil constitution, nor religious worship were dissolved, yet the power of life and death was taken from them; whereby he had an opportunity to publish the kingdom of the Messiah; that is, his own royalty, under the name of "the kingdom of God, and of heaven"; which the Jews well enough understood, and would certainly have put him to death for, had the power

been in their own hands. But this being no matter of accusation to the Romans, hindered him not from speaking of the kingdom of heaven, as he did: sometimes in reference to his appearing in the world, and being believed on by particular persons; sometimes in reference to the power that should be given him by the Father at the resurrection; and sometimes in reference to his coming to judge the world at the last day, in the full glory and completion of his kingdom. These were ways of declaring himself, which the Jews could lay no hold on, to bring him in danger with Pontius Pilate, and get him seized and put to death.

75. This being premised, let us take a view of the promulgation of the gospel by Our Saviour himself, and see what it was he taught the world, and required men to believe.

76. The first beginning of his ministry, whereby he shewed himself, seems to be at Cana in Galilee, soon after his baptism; where he turned water into wine, of which St. John, Ch. ii. 11, says thus: "This beginning of miracles Jesus made and manifested his glory, and his disciples believed in him." His disciples here believed in him, but we hear not of any other preaching to them, but by this miracle, whereby he manifested his glory, i.e. of being the Messiah the Prince. So Nathanael, without any other preaching, but only our Saviour's discovering to him that he knew him after an extraordinary manner, presently acknowledges him to be the Messiah; crying, "Rabbi, thou art the Son of God; thou art the king of Israel."

78. This, therefore, we may look on, in the beginning, as a pattern of Christ's preaching, and shewing himself to the Jews, which he generally followed afterwards; viz. such a manifestation of himself, as every one at present could not understand; but yet carried such an evidence with it, to those who were well-disposed now, or would reflect on it when the whole course of his ministry was over, as was sufficient clearly to convince them, that he was the Messiah.

139. One thing more there is, that gives us light into this wise and necessarily cautious management of himself, which manifestly agrees with it, and makes a part of it: and that is, the choice of his apostles; exactly suited to the design and foresight of the necessity of keeping the declaration of the kingdom of the Messiah, which was not expected, within certain general terms, during his ministry. It was not fit to open himself too plainly or forwardly to the heady Jews, that he himself was

the Messiah; that was to be left to be found out by the observation of those who would attend to the purity of his life, the testimony of his miracles, and the conformity of all with the predictions concerning him; by these marks, those he lived amongst were to find it out, without an express promulgation that he was the Messiah, till after his death: His kingdom was to be opened to them by degrees, as well to prepare them to receive it, as to enable him to be long enough amongst them, to perform what was the work of the Messiah, to be done; and fulfil all those several parts of what was foretold of him in the Old Testament, and we see applied to him in the New.

(140) The Jews had no other thoughts of their Messiah, but of a mighty temporal prince, that should raise their nation into an higher degree of power, dominion and prosperity, than ever it had enjoyed. They were filled with the expectation of a glorious earthly kingdom. It was not, therefore, for a poor man, the son of a carpenter, and (as they thought) born in Galilee, to pretend to it. None of the Jews, no, not his disciples could have borne this, if he had expressly avowed this at first, and began his preaching, and the opening of his kingdom this way, especially if he had added to it, that in a year or two, he should die an ignominious death upon the cross. They are therefore prepared for the truth by degrees.

142. Whether twelve other men, of quicker parts, and of a station or breeding, which might have given them any opinion of themselves, or their own abilities, would have been so easily kept from meddling, beyond just what was prescribed them, in a matter they had so much interest in; and have said nothing of what they might, in human prudence, have thought would have contributed to their master's reputation, and made way for his advancement to his kingdom, I leave to be considered. And it may suggest matter of meditation, whether St. Paul was not for this reason, by his learning, parts, and warmer temper, better fitted for an apostle after, than during our Saviour's ministry: and therefore, though a chosen vessel, was not by the divine wisdom called till after Christ's resurrection.

143. I offer this only as a subject of magnifying the admirable contrivance of the divine wisdom, in the whole work of our redemption, as far as we are able to trace it, by the footsteps which God hath made visible to human reason. For though it be as easy to omnipotent power to do all things by an immediate over-ruling will, and so to make any

instruments work, even contrary to their natures, in subserviency to his ends; yet his wisdom is not usually at the expense of miracles, (if I may so say) but only in cases that require them, for the evidencing of some revelation or mission to be from him. He does constantly (unless where the confirmation of some truth requires it otherwise) bring about his purposes by means operating according to their natures. If it were not so, the course and evidence of things would be confounded, miracles would lose their name and force; and there could be no distinction between natural and supernatural.

144. There had been no room left to see and admire the wisdom, as well as innocence of Our Saviour, if he had rashly every where exposed himself to the fury of the Jews, and had always been preserved by a miraculous suspension of their malice, or a miraculous rescuing him out of their hands. It was enough for him once to escape from the men of Nazareth, who were going to throw him down a precipice, for him never to preach to them again. Our Saviour had multitudes that followed him for the loaves, who barely seeing the miracles that he did, would have made him king. If to the miracles he did, he had openly added, in express words, that he was the Messiah, and the king they expected to deliver them, he would have had more followers, and warmer in the cause, and readier to set him up at the head of a tumult. These indeed God, by a miraculous influence, might have hindered from any such attempt; but then posterity could not have believed that the nation of the Jews did at that time expect the Messiah, their king and deliverer; or that Jesus, who declared himself to be that king and deliverer, shewed any miracles amongst them, to convince them of it; or did any thing worthy to make him be credited or received. If he had gone about preaching to the multitude which he drew after him, that he was the Messiah, the King of Israel, and this had been evidenced to Pilate, God could indeed, by a supernatural influence upon his mind, have made Pilate pronounce him innocent, and not condemn him as a malefactor, who had openly, for three years together, preached sedition to the people, and endeavoured to persuade them that he was the Messiah their king, of the blood-royal of David, come to deliver them. But then I ask, whether posterity would not either have suspected the story, or that some art had been used to gain that testimony from Pilate? Because he could not (for nothing) have been so favourable to Jesus, as to be willing to release

so turbulent and seditious a man; to declare him innocent, and to cast the blame and guilt of his death, as unjust, upon the envy of the Jews.

145. But now, the malice of the chief priests, scribes and Pharisees; the headiness of the mob, animated with hopes, and raised with miracles; Judas's treachery, and Pilate's care of his government, and of the peace of his province, all working naturally as they should; Jesus, by the admirable wariness of his carriage, and an extraordinary wisdom, visible in his whole conduct, weathers all these difficulties, does the work he comes for, uninterruptedly goes about preaching his full appointed time, sufficiently manifests himself to be the Messiah, in all the particulars the Scriptures had foretold of him; and when his hour is come, suffers death: but is acknowledged, both by Judas that betrayed, and Pilate that condemned him, to die innocent. For, to use his own words, Luke xxiv. 46, "Thus it is written, and thus it behoved the Messiah to suffer." And of his whole conduct, we have a reason and clear resolution in those words to St. Peter, Matt. xxvi. 53, "Thinkest thou that I cannot now pray to my Father, and he shall presently give me more than twelve legions of angels? But how then shall the scriptures be fulfilled, that thus it must be?"

(146) Having this clue to guide us, let us now observe, how Our Saviour's preaching and conduct comported with it in the last scene of his life.

158. To conclude all, in his prayer, which shuts up [the last discourse to his disciples], he tells the Father what he had made known to his apostles; the result whereof we have, John xvii. 8, "I have given unto them the words which thou gavest me, and they have received them, and THEY HAVE BELIEVED THAT THOU DIDST SEND ME." Which is in effect, that he was the Messiah promised and sent by God. And then he prays for them, and adds, vers. 20, 21, "Neither pray I for these alone, but for them also who believe on me through their word." What that word was through which others should believe in him, we have seen in the preaching of the apostles all through the history of the Acts, viz. This one great point, that Jesus was the Messiah. The apostles, he says, ver. 25, "know that thou hast sent me"; i.e. are assured that I am the Messiah. And in verses 21 and 23 he prays, "That the world may believe" (which ver. 23 is called knowing) "that thou hast sent me": So that what Christ would have believed by his disciples, we may see

by this his last prayer for them, when he was leaving the world, as well as by what he preached whilst he was in it.

159. And, as a testimony of this, one of his last actions, even when he was upon the cross, was to confirm his doctrine, by giving salvation to one of the thieves that was crucified with him, upon his declaration, that he believed him to be the Messiah: for so much the words of his request imported, when he said, "Remember me, Lord, when thou comest into thy kingdom", Luke xxiii. 42. To which Jesus replied, ver. 43, "Verily I say unto thee, today shalt thou be with me in paradise." An expression very remarkable: for as Adam, by sin, lost paradise, i.e. a state of happy immortality; here the believing thief, through his faith in Jesus the Messiah, is promised to be put in paradise, and so reinstated in an happy immortality.

(160) Thus Our Saviour ended his life. And what he did after his resurrection, St. Luke tells us, Acts i. 3, that he shewed himself to the apostles "forty days, speaking things concerning the kingdom of God". This was what Our Saviour preached in the whole course of his ministry, before his passion: and no other mysteries of faith does he now discover to them after his resurrection.

164. To this, 'tis likely, it will be objected by some, that to believe only that Jesus of Nazareth is the Messiah, is but an historical, and not a justifying, or saving faith.

165. To which I answer, that I allow to the makers of systems and their followers, to invent and use what distinctions they please, and to call things by what names they think fit. But I cannot allow to them, or to any man, an authority to make a religion for me, or to alter that which God hath revealed. And if they please to call the believing that which Our Saviour and his apostles preached and proposed alone to be believed, an historical faith, they have their liberty, but they must have a care how they deny it to be a justifying or saving faith, when Our Saviour and his apostles have declared it so to be, and taught no other which men should receive, and whereby they should be made believers unto eternal life; unless they can so far make bold with Our Saviour, for the sake of their beloved systems, as to say, that he forgot what he came into the world for; and that he and his apostles did not instruct people right in the way and mysteries of salvation. For that this is the sole doctrine pressed and required to be believed in the whole tenor of Our Saviour's and his apostles preaching, we have shewed through the

whole history of the evangelists and the Acts. And I challenge them to shew, that there was any other doctrine, upon their assent to which, or disbelief of it, men were pronounced believers or unbelievers; and accordingly received into the Church of Christ, as members of his Body, as far as mere believing could make them so, or else kept out of it. This was the only gospel-article of faith which was preached to them. And if nothing else was preached every where, the apostle's argument will hold against any other articles of faith to be believed under the gospel, Rom. x. 14, "How shall they believe that whereof they have not heard?" For to preach any other doctrines necessary to be believed, we do not find that anybody was sent.

166. Perhaps it will farther be argued, that this is not a "saving faith"; because such a faith as this the devils may have, and 'twas plain they had; for they believed and declared Jesus to be the Messiah. And St. James, Ch. ii. 19, tells us, "The devils believe, and tremble"; and yet they shall not be saved. To which I answer, 1. That they could not be saved by any faith, to whom it was not proposed as a means of salvation, nor ever promised to be counted for righteousness. This was an act of grace, shewn only to mankind. God dealt so favourably with the posterity of Adam, that if they would believe Jesus to be the Messiah, the promised King and Saviour, and perform what other conditions were required of them by the covenant of grace, God would justify them because of this belief; he would account this faith to them for righteousness, and look on it as making up the defects of their obedience; which being thus supplied by what was taken instead of it, they were looked on as just or righteous, and so inherited eternal life. But this favour shewn to mankind, was never offered to the fallen angels. They had no such proposals made to them; and therefore whatever of this kind was proposed to men, it availed not devils whatever they performed of it. The covenant of grace was never offered to them.

(167) 2. I answer; that though the devils believed, yet they could not be saved by the covenant of grace; because they performed not the other condition required in it, altogether as necessary to be performed as this of believing: and that is repentance. Repentance is as absolute a condition of the covenant of grace as faith; and as necessary to be performed as that.

172. These two, faith and repentance, i.e. believing Jesus to be the

Messiah, and a good life, are the indispensable conditions of the new covenant, to be performed by all those who would obtain eternal life. The reasonableness, or rather necessity of which, that we may the better comprehend, we must a little look back to what was said in the beginning.

173. Adam being the son of God, and so St. Luke calls him, Ch. iii. 38, had this part also of the likeness and image of his father, viz. that he was immortal. But Adam transgressing the command given him by his heavenly Father, incurred the penalty, forfeited that state of immortality, and became mortal. After this, Adam begot children: but they were "in his own likeness, after his own image"; mortal, like their father.

(174) God nevertheless, out of his infinite mercy, willing to bestow eternal life on mortal men, sends Jesus Christ into the world; who being conceived in the womb of a virgin (that had not known man) by the immediate power of God, was properly the Son of God.

(178) God therefore, out of his mercy to mankind, and for the erecting of the kingdom of his Son, and furnishing it with subjects out of every kindred, and tongue, and people, and nation, proposed to the children of men, that as many of them as would believe Jesus his Son (whom he sent into the world) to be the Messiah, the promised Deliverer; and would receive him for their King and Ruler; should have all their past sins, disobedience, and rebellion forgiven them: and if for the future they lived in a sincere obedience to his law, to the utmost of their power; the sins of human frailty for the time to come, as well as all those of their past lives, should, for his Son's sake, because they gave themselves up to him, to be his subjects, be forgiven them; and so their faith, which made them be baptized into his name (i.e. enrol themselves in the kingdom of Jesus the Messiah, and profess themselves his subjects, and consequently live by the laws of his kingdom) should be accounted to them for righteousness; i.e. should supply the defects of a scanty obedience in the sight of God; who, counting this faith to them for righteousness, or complete obedience, did thus justify, or make them just, and thereby capable of eternal life.

(179) [So] believing him to be the Messiah their King, it was further required, that those who would have the privilege, advantage and deliverance of his kingdom, should enter themselves into it; and by baptism being made denizens, and solemnly incorporated into that

kingdom, live as became subjects obedient to the laws of it. For if they believed him to be the Messiah, their King, but would not obey his laws, and would not have him to reign over them, they were but the greater rebels; and God would not justify them for a faith that did but increase their guilt, and oppose diametrically the kingdom and design of the Messiah; "Who gave himself for us, that he might redeem us from all iniquity, and purify unto himself a peculiar people, zealous of good works", Titus ii. 14. And therefore St. Paul tells the Galatians, that that which availeth is faith; but faith working by love. And that faith without works, i.e. the works of sincere obedience to the law and will of Christ, is not sufficient for our justification, St. James shews at large, Ch. ii.

180. Neither, indeed, could it be otherwise; for life, eternal life being the reward of justice or righteousness only, appointed by the righteous God (who is of purer eyes than to behold iniquity) to those only who had no taint or infection of sin upon them, it is impossible that he should justify those who had no regard to justice at all, whatever they believed. This would have been to encourage iniquity, contrary to the purity of his nature, and to have condemned that eternal law of right, which is holy, just, and good: of which no one precept or rule is abrogated or repealed; nor indeed can be, whilst God is an holy, just, and righteous God, and man a rational creature. The duties of that law arising from the constitution of his very nature, are of eternal obligation; nor can it be taken away, or dispensed with, without changing the nature of things, or overturning the measures of right and wrong, and thereby introducing and authorizing irregularity, confusion, and disorder in the world. Christ's coming into the world was not for such an end as that; but on the contrary, to reform the corrupt state of degenerate man; and out of those who would mend their lives, and bring forth fruit meet for repentance, erect a new kingdom.

181. This is the law of that kingdom, as well as of all mankind; and that law, by which all men shall be judged at the last day. Only those who have believed Jesus to be the Messiah, and have taken him to be their King, with a sincere endeavour after righteousness, in obeying his law, shall have their past sins not imputed to them; and shall have that faith taken instead of obedience, where frailty and weakness made them transgress, and sin prevailed after conversion, in those who hunger and thirst after righteousness (or perfect obedience), and do not

allow themselves in acts of disobedience and rebellion, against the laws of that kingdom they are entered into.

182. He did not expect, 'tis true, a perfect obedience, void of slips and falls: he knew our make, and the weakness of our condition too well, and was sent with a supply for that defect. Besides, perfect obedience was the righteousness of the law of works; and then the reward would be of debt, and not of grace: And to such there was no need of faith to be imputed to them for righteousness. They stood upon their own legs, were just already, and needed no allowance to be made them for believing Jesus to be the Messiah, taking him for their King, and becoming his subjects. But that Christ does require obedience, sincere obedience, is evident from the laws he himself delivers (unless he can be supposed to give and inculcate laws, only to have them disobeyed) and from the sentence he will pass, when he comes to judge.

184. What those were to do, who believed him to be the Messiah, and received him for their King, that they might be admitted to be partakers with him of his kingdom in glory, we shall best know by the laws he gives them, and requires them to obey; and by the sentence which he himself will give, when, sitting on his throne, they shall all appear at his tribunal, to receive every one his doom from the mouth of this righteous Judge of all men.

185. What he proposes to his followers to be believed, we have already seen, by examining his, and his apostles' preaching, step by step, all through the history of the four evangelists, and the Acts of the apostles. The same method will best and plainest shew us, whether he required of those who believed him to be the Messiah, any thing besides that faith, and what it was. For, he being a King, we shall see by his commands what he expects from his subjects: for, if he did not expect obedience to them, his commands would be but mere mockery; and if there were no punishment for the transgressors of them, his laws would not be the laws of a king, that had no authority to command, and power to chastise the disobedient; but empty talk, without force, and without influence.

186. We shall therefore from his injunctions (if any such there be) see what he has made necessary to be performed, by all those who shall be received into eternal life, in his kingdom prepared in the heavens. And in this we cannot be deceived. What we have from his own mouth,

especially if repeated over and over again, in different places and expressions, will be past doubt and controversy. I shall pass by all that is said by St. John Baptist, or any other before our Saviour's entry upon his ministry, and public promulgation of the laws of his kingdom.

187. He began his preaching with a command to repent, as St. Matthew tells us, iv. 17, "From that time Jesus began to preach; saying, Repent, for the Kingdom of Heaven is at hand." And Luke v. 32, he tells the scribes and Pharisees, "I come not to call the righteous" (those who were truly so, needed no help, they had a right to the tree of life), "but sinners to repentance."

(188) In his sermon, as 'tis called, in the mount, Luke vi. and Matt. v, etc., he commands they should be exemplary in good works: "Let your light so shine amongst men, that they may see your good works, and glorify your Father which is in heaven", Matt. v. 16. And that they might know what he came for, and what he expected of them, he tells them, vers. 17–20, "Think not that I am come to dissolve", or loosen, "the law, or the prophets: I am not come to dissolve", or loosen, "but to make it full", or complete; by giving it you in its true and strict sense. Here we see he confirms, and at once reinforces all the moral precepts in the Old Testament. In the following part of his sermon, which is to be read Luke vi, and more at large, Matt. v, vi, vii, he not only forbids actual uncleanness, but all irregular desires, upon pain of hell-fire; causeless divorces; swearing in conversation, as well as forswearing in judgment; revenge, retaliation; ostentation of charity, of devotion, and of fasting; repetitions in prayer, covetousness, worldly care, censoriousness: and on the other side, commands loving our enemies, doing good to those that hate us, praying for those that despitefully use us; patience and meekness under injuries, forgiveness, liberality, compassion: and closes all his particular injunctions, with this general golden rule, Matt. vii. 12, "All things whatsoever ye would have that men should do to you, do ye even so to them. For this is the Law and the Prophets." And to show how much he is in earnest, and expects obedience to these Laws; he tells . . . disobedient subjects [that] though they have prophesied and done miracles in [his] name, [he will] say at the day of judgment, "Depart from me, ye workers of iniquity; I know you not."

212. Thus we see Our Saviour not only confirmed the moral law; and clearing it from the corrupt glories of the scribes and Pharisees,

shewed the strictness, as well as obligation of its injunctions; but more-over, upon occasion, requires the obedience of his disciples to several of the commands be afresh lays upon them; with the inforcement of unspeakable rewards and punishments in another world, according to their obedience or disobedience. There is not, I think, any of the duties of morality, which he has not, somewhere or other, by himself and his apostles, inculcated over and over again to his followers in express terms. And is it for nothing, that he is so instant with them to bring forth fruit? Does he their King command, and is it an indifferent thing? Or will their happiness or misery not at all depend upon it, whether they obey or no? They were required to believe him to be the Messiah; which faith is of grace promised to be reckoned to them for the completing of their righteousness, wherein it was defective: But righteousness, or obedience to the law of God, was their great business, which, if they could have attained by their own performances, there would have been no need of this gracious allowance in reward of their faith; but eternal life, after the resurrection, had been their due by a former covenant, even that of works, the rule whereof was never abolished, though the rigour was abated. The duties enjoined in it were duties still: their obligations had never ceased, nor a wilful neglect of them was ever dispensed with; but their past transgressions were pardoned, to those who received Jesus, the promised Messiah, for their King; and their future slips covered, if, renouncing their former iniquities, they entered into his kingdom, and continued his subjects, with a steady resolution and endeavour to obey his laws. This righteous-ness therefore, a complete obedience and freedom from sin, are still sincerely to be endeavoured after: and 'tis nowhere promised, that those who persist in a wilful disobedience to his laws, shall be received into the eternal bliss of his kingdom, how much soever they believe in him.

213. A sincere obedience, how can any one doubt to be, or scruple to call, a condition of the new covenant, as well as faith; whoever read Our Saviour's sermon in the mount, to omit all the rest? Can any thing be more express than these words of Our Lord? Matt. vi. 14, "If you forgive men their trespasses, your heavenly Father will also forgive you; but if ye forgive not men their trespasses, neither will your Father forgive your trespasses." And John xiii. 17, "If ye know these things, happy are ye if ye do them." This is so indispensable a condition

of the new covenant, that believing without it, will not do, nor be accepted, if Our Saviour knew the terms on which he would admit men into life. "Why call ye me Lord, Lord", says he, Luke vi. 46, "and do not the things which I say?" It is not enough to believe him to be the Messiah, the Lord, without obeying him: For that these he speaks to here were believers, is evident from the parallel place, Matt. vii. 21–23, where it is thus recorded: "Not every one who says Lord, Lord, shall enter into the kingdom of heaven; but he that doeth the will of my Father, which is in heaven." No rebels, or refractory disobedient, shall be admitted there, though they have so far believed in Jesus, as to be able to do miracles in his name; as is plain out of the following words, "Many will say to me in that day, Have we not prophesied in thy name, and in thy name have cast out devils, and in thy name have done many wonderful works? And then will I profess unto them, I never knew you: depart from me, ye workers of iniquity."

214. This part of the new covenant, the apostles also, in their preaching the gospel of the Messiah, ordinarily joined with the doctrine of faith.

220. Thus we see, by the preaching of Our Saviour and his apostles, that he required of those who believed him to be the Messiah, and received him for their Lord and Deliverer, that they should live by his laws: and that (though in consideration of their becoming his subjects, by faith in him, whereby they believed and took him to be the Messiah, their former sins should be forgiven) yet he would own none to be his, nor receive them as true denizens of the new Jerusalem, into the inheritance of eternal life; but leave them to the condemnation of the unrighteous who renounced not their former miscarriages, and lived in a sincere obedience to his commands. What he expects from his followers, he has sufficiently declared as a Legislator: and that they may not be deceived, by mistaking the doctrine of faith, grace, free-grace, and the pardon and forgiveness of sins, and salvation by him (which was the great end of his coming), he more than once declares to them, for what omissions and miscarriages he shall judge and condemn to death, even those who have owned him, and done miracles in his name: when he comes at last to render to every one according to what he had done in the flesh, sitting upon his great and glorious tribunal, at the end of the world.

221. The first place where we find Our Saviour to have mentioned

the day of judgment, is John v. 28, 29, in these words: "The hour is coming, in which all that are in their graves shall hear his [i.e. the Son of God's] voice, and shall come forth, they that have DONE GOOD, unto the resurrection of life, and they that have DONE EVIL, unto the resurrection of damnation." That which puts the distinction, if we will believe Our Saviour, is the having done good or evil. And he gives a reason of the necessity of his judging or condemning those who have done evil, in the following words, ver. 30, "I can of my own self do nothing. As I hear I judge, and my judgment is just; because I seek not my own will, but the will of my Father who hath sent me." He could not judge of himself; he had but a delegated power of judging from the Father, whose will he obeyed in it, and who was of purer eyes than to admit any unjust person into the kingdom of heaven.

222. Matt. vii. 22, 23, speaking again of that day, he tells what his sentence will be, "Depart from me, ye WORKERS of iniquity." Faith, in the penitent and sincerely obedient, supplies the defect of their performances, and so by grace they are made just. But we may observe, none are sentenced or punished for unbelief, but only for their misdeeds. They are "workers of iniquity" on whom the sentence is pronounced.

223. Matt. xiii. 40, "At the end of the world, the Son of man shall send forth his angels; and they shall gather out of his kingdom all scandals, and them which DO INIQUITY; and cast them into a furnace of fire; there shall be wailing and gnashing of teeth." And again, ver. 49, "The angels shall sever the WICKED from among the JUST; and shall cast them into the furnace of fire."

224. Matt. xvi. 27, "For the Son of man shall come in the glory of his Father, with his angels: and then he shall reward every man according to his WORKS."

225. Luke xiii. 26, "Then shall ye begin to say, We have eaten and drank in the presence, and thou hast taught in our streets. But he shall say, I tell you, I know you not; depart from me, ye workers of iniquity."

226. Matt. xxv. 31–46, "When the Son of man shall come in his glory; and before him shall be gathered all nations; he shall set the sheep on his right hand, and the goats on his left. Then shall the King say to them on his right-hand, Come, ye blessed of my Father, inherit the kingdom prepared for you from the foundation of the world: For I was an hungered, and ye gave me meat; I was thirsty, and ye gave me drink; I was a stranger, and ye took me in; naked, and ye

clothed me; I was sick, and ye visited me; I was in prison, and ye came unto me. Then shall the righteous answer him, saying, Lord, when saw we thee an hungered, and fed thee? etc. And the King shall answer, and say unto them, Verily, I say unto you, inasmuch as ye have done it unto one of the least of these my brethren, ye have done it unto me. Then shall he say unto them on the left-hand, Depart from me, ye cursed, into everlasting fire, prepared for the devil and his angels: For I was an hungered, and ye gave me no meat; I was thirsty, and ye gave me no drink; I was a stranger, and ye took me not in; naked, and ye clothed me not; sick and in prison, and ye visited me not. Insomuch that ye did it not to one of these, ye did it not to me. And these shall go into everlasting punishment: but the righteous into life eternal."

227. These, I think, are all the places where Our Saviour mentions the last judgment, or describes his way of proceeding in that great day; wherein, as we have observed, it is remarkable, that every where the sentence follows, doing or not doing; without any mention of believing, or not believing. Not that any to whom the gospel hath been preached shall be saved, without believing Jesus to be the Messiah; for all being sinners, and transgressors of the law, and so unjust, are all liable to condemnation, unless they believe, and so through grace are justified by God for this faith, which shall be accounted to them for righteousness: but the rest wanting this cover, this allowance for their transgressions, must answer for all their actions; and being found transgressors of the law, shall, by the letter and sanction of that law, be condemned, for not having paid a full obedience to that law, and not for want of faith; that is not the guilt, on which the punishment is laid; though it be the want of faith, which lays open their guilt un-covered; and exposes them to the sentence of the law, against all that are unrighteous.

(228) The common objection here, is: if all sinners shall be con-demned, but such as have a gracious allowance made them; and so are justified by God, for believing Jesus to be the Messiah, and so taking him for their King; whom they are resolved to obey, to the utmost of their power, "What shall become of all mankind, who lived before Our Saviour's time; who never heard of his name, and consequently could not believe in him?" To this the answer is so obvious and natural, that one would wonder how any reasonable man should think it worth the urging. No body was, or can be, required to believe, what

was never proposed to him to believe. Before the fullness of time, which God from the counsel of his own wisdom had appointed to send his Son in, he had, at several times, and in different manners, promised to the people of Israel, an extraordinary person to come; who, raised from amongst themselves, should be their Ruler and Deliverer. The time, and other circumstances of his birth, life, and person, he had in sundry prophecies so particularly described, and so plainly foretold, that he was well known, and expected by the Jews, under the name of the Messiah, or Anointed, given him in some of these prophecies. All then that was required, before his appearing in the world, was to believe what God had revealed, and to rely with a full assurance on God, for the performance of his promise; and believe that in due time he would send them the Messiah, this anointed King, this promised Saviour and Deliverer, according to his word. This faith in the promises of God, this relying and acquiescing in his word and faithfulness, the Almighty takes well at our hands, as a great mark of homage, paid by us poor frail creatures, to his goodness and truth, as well as to his power: and wisdom; and accepts it as an acknowledgement of his peculiar providence, and benignity to us. And therefore, Our Saviour tells us, John xii. 44, "He that believes on me, believes not on me, but on him that sent me." The works of nature shew his wisdom and power; but 'tis his peculiar care of mankind, most eminently discovered in his promises to them, that shews his bounty and goodness; and consequently engages their hearts in love and affection to him. This obligation of an heart, fixed with dependence on, and affection to him, is the most acceptable tribute we can pay him, the foundation of true devotion and life of all religion. What a value he puts on this depending on his word, and resting satisfied on his promises, we have an example in Abraham; whose faith "was counted to him for righteousness", as we have before remarked out of Rom. iv. And his relying firmly on the promise of God, without any doubt of its performance, gave him the name of the father of the faithful; and gained him so much favour with the Almighty, that he was called the "friend of God"; the highest and most glorious title can be bestowed on a creature.

229. The examples of faith, which St. Paul enumerates and proposed in the following words, [Heb.] Ch. xi, plainly shew, that the faith, whereby those believers of old pleased God, was nothing but a steadfast

reliance on the goodness and faithfulness of God, for those good things, which either the light of nature, or particular promises, had given them grounds to hope for. Of what avail this faith was with God, we may see, ver. 4, "By faith Abel offered unto God a more excellent sacrifice than Cain; by which he obtained witness that he was righteous." Ver. 5, "By faith Enoch was translated, that he should not see death: for before his translation he had this testimony, that he pleased God." Ver. 7, "Noah, being warned of God of things not seen as yet", being wary, "by faith prepared an Ark, to the saving of his house; by the which he condemned the world, and became heir of the righteousness which is by faith." And what it was that God so graciously accepted and rewarded, we are told, ver. 11, "Through faith also Sarah herself received strength to conceive seed, and was delivered of a child, when she was past age." How she came to obtain this grace from God, the apostle tells us; "Because she judged him faithful who had promised." Those therefore who pleased God, and were accepted by him before the coming of Christ, did it only by believing the promises, and relying on the goodness of God, as far as he had revealed it to them. For the apostle, in the following words, tells us, ver. 13, "These all died in faith, not having received" (the accomplishment of) "the promises; but having seen them afar off: and were persuaded of them, and embraced them." This was all that was required of them to be persuaded of, and embrace the promises which they had. They could be persuaded of no more than was proposed to them; embrace no more than was revealed, according to the promises they had received, and the dispensations they were under. And if the faith of things "seen afar off;" if their trusting in God for the promises he then gave them; if a belief of the Messiah to come, were sufficient to render those who lived in the ages before Christ, acceptable to God, and righteous before him: I desire those who tell us, that God will not (nay, some go so far as to say, cannot accept) any, who do not believe every article of their particular creeds and systems, to consider, why God, out of his infinite mercy, cannot as well justify man now, for believing Jesus of Nazareth to be the promised Messiah, the King and Deliverer, as those heretofore, who believed only that God would, according to his promise, in due time send the Messiah, to be a King and Deliverer.

230. There is another difficulty often to be met with, which seems to have something of more weight in it: and that is, that "though the

faith of those before Christ (believing that God would send the Messiah, to be a Prince, and a Saviour to his people, as he had promised), and the faith of those since his time (believing Jesus to be that Messiah, promised and sent by God), shall be accounted to them for righteousness; yet what shall become of all the rest of mankind, who, having never heard of the promise or news of a Saviour, not a word of a Messiah to be sent, or that was come, have had no thought or belief concerning him?"

231. To this I answer; that God will require of every man, "according to what a man hath, and not according to what he hath not". He will not expect ten talents where he gave but one; nor require any one should believe a promise, of which he has never heard. The apostle's reasoning, Rom. x. 14, is very just: "How shall they believe in him, of whom they have not heard?" But though there be many, who being strangers to the commonwealth of Israel, were also strangers to the oracles of God committed to that people; many, to whom the promise of the Messiah never came, and so were never in a capacity to believe or reject that revelation; yet God had, by the light of reason, revealed to all mankind, who would make use of that light, that he was good and merciful. The same spark of the divine nature and knowledge in man, which making him a man, shewed him the law he was under as a man; shewed him also the way of atoning the merciful, kind, compassionate Author and Father of him and his being, when he had transgressed that law. He that made use of this candle of the Lord, so far as to find what was his duty, could not miss to find also the way to reconciliation and forgiveness, when he had failed of his duty: though, if he used not his reason this way, if he put out or neglected this light, he might, perhaps, see neither.

232. The law is the eternal, immutable standard of right. And a part of that law is, that a man should forgive, not only his children, but his enemies, upon their repentance, asking pardon, and amendment. And therefore he could not doubt that the author of this law, and God of patience and consolation, who is rich in mercy, would forgive his frail offspring, if they acknowledged their faults, disapproved the iniquity of their transgressions, begged his pardon, and resolved in earnest for the future to conform their actions to this rule, which they owned to be just and right. This way of reconciliation, this hope of atonement, the light of nature revealed to them: and the revelation of

the gospel, having said nothing to the contrary, leaves them to stand and fall to their own Father and Master, whose goodness and mercy is over all his works.

233. I know some are forward to urge that place of the Acts, Ch. iv, as contrary to this. The words, vers. 10 and 12, stand thus: "Be it known unto you all, and to all the people of Israel, that by the name of Jesus Christ of Nazareth, whom ye crucified, whom God raised from the dead, even by him, doth this man" (i.e. the lame man restored by Peter) "stand here before you whole. This is the stone which is set at nought by you builders, which is become the head of the corner. Neither is there salvation in any other: for there is none other name under heaven given among men, in which we must be saved." Which, in short, is, that Jesus is the only true Messiah, neither is there any other person, but he, given to be a mediator between God and man, in whose name we may ask, and hope for salvation.

234. It will here possibly be asked, "Quorsum perditio hæc?" What need was there of a Saviour? What advantage have we by Jesus Christ?

235. It is enough to justify the fitness of any thing to be done, by resolving it into the "wisdom of God", who has done it; though our short views, and narrow understandings, may utterly incapacitate us to see that wisdom, and to judge rightly of it. We know little of this visible, and nothing at all of the state of that intellectual world, wherein are infinite numbers and degrees of spirits out of the reach of our ken or guess; and therefore know not what transactions there were between God and Our Saviour, in reference to his kingdom. We know not what need there was to set up a head and a chieftain, in opposition to the prince of this world, the prince of the power of the air, etc., whereof there are more than obscure intimations in Scripture. And we shall take too much upon us, if we shall call God's wisdom, or providence to account, and pertly condemn for needless, all that our weak, and perhaps biassed understanding, cannot account for.

236. Though this general answer be reply enough to the fore-mentioned demand, and such as a rational man, or fair searcher after truth, will acquiesce in; yet in this particular case, the wisdom and goodness of God has shewn himself so visibly to common apprehensions, that it hath furnished us abundantly wherewithal to satisfy the curious and inquisitive, who will not take a blessing, unless they be

instructed what need they had of it, and why it was bestowed upon them. The great and many advantages we receive by the coming of Jesus the Messiah, will shew, that it was not without need, that he was sent into the world.

237. The evidence of Our Saviour's mission from heaven is so great, in the multitude of miracles he did, before all sorts of people, that what he delivered cannot but be received as the oracles of God, and unquestionable verity. For the miracles he did were so ordered by the divine providence and wisdom, that they never were, nor could be denied by any of the enemies or opposers of Christianity.

238. Though the works of nature, in every part of them, sufficiently evidence a Deity; yet the world made so little use of their reason, that they saw him not, where, even by the impressions of himself, he was easy to be found. Sense and lust blinded their minds in some, and a careless inadvertency in others, and fearful apprehensions in most (who either believed there were, or could not but suspect there might be, superior unknown beings) gave them up into the hands of their priests, to fill their heads with false notions of the deity, and their worship with foolish rites, as they pleased; and what dread or craft once began, devotion soon made sacred, and religion immutable. In this state of darkness and ignorance of the true God, vice and superstition held the world; nor could any help be had or hoped for from reason, which could not be heard, and was judged to have nothing to do in the case: the priests every where, to secure their empire, having excluded reason from having anything to do in religion. And in the crowd of wrong notions, and invented rites, the world had almost lost the sight of the one only true God. The rational and thinking part of mankind, 'tis true, when they sought after him, found the one, supreme, invisible God: but if they acknowledged and worshipped him, it was only in their own minds. They kept this truth locked up in their own breasts as a secret, nor ever durst venture it amongst the people, much less the priests, those wary guardians of their own creeds and profitable inventions. Hence we see that reason, speaking never so clearly to the wise and virtuous, had ever authority enough to prevail on the multitude, and to persuade the societies of men, that there was but one God, that alone was to be owned and worshipped. The belief and worship of one God, was the national religion of the Israelites alone; and, if we will consider it, it was introduced and supported amongst that people

by revelation. They were in Goshen, and had light, whilst the rest of the world were in almost Egyptian darkness, without God in the world. There was no part of mankind, who had quicker parts, or improved them more; that had a greater light of reason, or followed it farther in all sorts of speculations, than the Athenians, and yet we find but one Socrates amongst them, that opposed and laughed at their polytheisms, and wrong opinions of the deity; and we see how they rewarded him for it. Whatsoever Plato, and the soberest of the philosophers thought of the nature and being of the one God, they were fain, in their outward worship, to go with the herd, and keep to the religion established by law; which what it was, and how it had disposed the mind of these knowing and quicksighted Grecians, St. Paul tells us, Acts xvii. 22–29, "Ye men of Athens," says he, "I perceive that in all things ye are too superstitious. For as I passed by, and beheld your devotions, I found an altar with this inscription, TO THE UNKNOWN GOD. Whom therefore ye ignorantly worship, him declare I unto you. God that made the world, and all things therein, seeing that he is Lord of heaven and earth, dwelleth not in temples made with hands: neither is worshipped with men's hands, as though he needed any thing, seeing he giveth unto all life, and breath, and all things; and hath made of one blood all the nations of men, for to dwell on the face of the earth; and hath determined the times before appointed, and the bounds of their habitations; that they should seek the Lord, if haply they might feel him out, and find him, though he be not far from every one of us." Here he tells the Athenians, that they, and the rest of the world (given up to superstition) whatever light there was in the works of creation and providence, to lead them to the true God, yet they few of them found him. He was every where near them; yet they were but like people groping and feeling for something in the dark, and did not see him with a full and clear day-light; "But thought the Godhead like to gold and silver, and stone, graven by art and man's device."

239. In this state of darkness and error, in reference to the "true God", Our Saviour found the world. But the clear revelation he brought with him, dissipated this darkness; made the one invisible true God known to the world: and that with such evidence and energy, that polytheism and idolatry hath no where been able to withstand it. But wherever the preaching of the truth he delivered, and the light of

the gospel hath come, those mists have been dispelled. And, in effect, we, see that since Our Saviour's time, the belief of one God has prevailed and spread itself over the face of the earth. For even to the light that the Messiah brought into the world with him, we must ascribe the owning, and profession of one God, which the Mahometan religion hath derived and borrowed from it. So that, in this sense, it is certainly and manifestly true of Our Saviour, what St. John says of him, 1 John iii. 8, "For this purpose the Son of God was manifested, that he might destroy the works of the devil." This light the world needed, and this light it received from him: that there is but "one God", and he "eternal, invisible;" nor like to any visible objects, nor to be represented by them.

240. If it be asked, whether the revelation to the patriarchs by Moses, did not teach this, and why that was not enough? The answer is obvious; that however clearly the knowledge of one invisible God, maker of heaven and earth, was revealed to them; yet that revelation was shut up in a little corner of the world, amongst a people, by that very law, which they received with it, excluded from a commerce and communication with the rest of mankind. The Gentile world, in Our Saviour's time, and several ages before, could have no attestation of the miracles, on which the Hebrews built their faith, but from the Jews themselves, a people not known to the greatest part of mankind, contemned and thought vilely of by those nations that did know them; and therefore very unfit and unable to propagate the doctrine of one God in the world, and diffuse it through the nations of the earth, by the strength and force of that ancient revelation, upon which they had received it. But Our Saviour, when he came, threw down this wall of partition, and did not confine his miracles or message to the land of Canaan, or the worshippers at Jerusalem; but he himself preached at Samaria, and did miracles in the borders of Tyre and Sidon, and before multitudes of people gathered from all quarters. And after his resurrection, sent his apostles amongst the nations, accompanied with miracles, which were done in all parts so frequently, and before so many witnesses of all sorts, in broad day-light, that, as I have before observed, the enemies of Christianity have never dared to deny them; No, not Julian himself, who neither wanted skill nor power to enquire into the truth, nor would have failed to have proclaimed and exposed it, if he could have detected any falsehood in the history of the gospel, or found

the least ground to question the matter of fact published of Christ, and his apostles. The number and evidence of the miracles done by Our Saviour and his followers, by the power and force of truth, bore down this mighty and accomplished emperor, and all his parts, in his own dominions. He durst not deny so plain matter of fact, which being granted, the truth of Our Saviour's doctrine and mission unavoidably follows; notwithstanding whatsoever artful suggestions his wit could invent, or malice should offer, to the contrary.

241. 2. Next to the knowledge of one God; maker of all things; a clear knowledge of their duty was wanting to mankind. This part of knowledge, though cultivated with some care, by some of the heathen philosophers, yet got little footing among the people. All men indeed, under pain of displeasing the gods, were to frequent the temples, every one went to their sacrifices and services; but the priests made it not their business to teach them virtue. If they were diligent in their observations and ceremonies, punctual in their feasts and solemnities, and the tricks of religion, the holy tribe assured them, the gods were pleased; and they looked no farther. Few went to the schools of the philosophers, to be instructed in their duties and to know what was good and evil in their action. The priests sold the better penny-worths, and therefore had all their custom. Lustrations and processions were much easier than a clean conscience, and a steady course of virtue; and an expiatory sacrifice, that atoned for the want of it, was much more convenient, than a strict and holy life. No wonder then, that religion was every where distinguished from, and preferred to virtue, and that it was dangerous heresy and prophaneness to think the contrary. So much virtue as was necessary to hold societies together, and to contribute to the quiet of governments, the civil laws of commonwealths taught, and forced upon men that lived under magistrates. But these laws, being for the most part made by such who had no other aims but their own power, reached no farther than those things, that would serve to tie men together in subjection; or at most, were directly to conduce to the prosperity and temporal happiness of any people. But natural religion, in its full extent, was nowhere, that I know, taken care of by the force of natural reason. It should seem, by the little that has hitherto been done in it, that 'tis too hard a task for unassisted reason, to establish morality, in all its parts, upon its true foundations, with a clear and convincing light. And 'tis at least a surer

and shorter way, to the apprehensions of the vulgar, and mass of mankind, that one manifestly sent from God, and coming with visible authority from him, should, as a King and law-maker, tell them their duties, and require their obedience, than leave it to the long, and sometimes intricate deductions of reason, to be made out to them: such strains of reasonings the greatest part of mankind have neither leisure to weigh, nor, for want of education and use, skill to judge of. We see how unsuccessful in this, the attempts of philosophers were, before Our Saviour's time. How short their several systems came of the perfection of a true and complete morality, is very visible. And if, since that, the Christian philosophers have much outdone them, yet we may observe, that the first knowledge of the truths they have added, are owing to revelation; though as soon as they are heard and considered, they are found to be agreeable to reason, and such as can by no means be contradicted. Every one may observe a great many truths which he receives at first from others, and readily assents to, as consonant to reason, which he would have found it hard, and perhaps, beyond his strength to have discovered himself. Native and original truth, is not so easily wrought out of the mine, as we who have it delivered, ready dug and fashioned into our hands, are apt to imagine. And how often at fifty or threescore years old, are thinking men told, what they wonder how they could miss thinking of? Which yet their own contemplations did not, and possibly never would have helped them to. Experience shews that the knowledge of morality, by mere natural light (how agreeable soever it be to it), makes but a slow progress, and little advance in the world. And the reason of it is not hard to be found in men's necessities, passions, vices, and mistaken interests, which turn their thoughts another way. And the designing leaders, as well as the following herd, find it not to their purpose to employ much of their meditations this way. Or whatever else was the cause, 'tis plain in fact, that human reason unassisted, failed men in its great and proper business of morality. It never, from unquestionable principles, by clear deductions, made out an entire body of the law of Nature. And he that shall collect all the moral rules of the philosophers, and compare them with those contained in the new testament, will find them to come short of the morality delivered by Our Saviour, and taught by his apostles; a college made up, for the most part, of ignorant, but inspired fishermen.

242. Though yet, if any one should think, that out of the saying of the wise heathens, before Our Saviour's time, there might be a collection made of all those rules of morality, which are to be found in the Christian religion; yet this would not at all hinder, but that the world, nevertheless, stood as much in need of Our Saviour, and the morality delivered by him. Let it be granted (though not true) that all the moral precepts of the gospel were known by some body or other, amongst mankind, before. But where, or how, or of what use, is not considered. Suppose they may be picked up here and there; some from Solon and Bias in Greece; others from Tully in Italy; and, to complete the work, let Confucius, as far as China, be consulted; and Anacharsis the Scythian contribute his share. What will all this do, to give the world a complete morality, that may be to mankind, the unquestionable rule of life and manners? I will not here urge the impossibility of collecting from men, so far distant from one another, in time, and place, and languages. I will suppose there was a Stobæus in those times, who had gathered the moral sayings from all the sages of the world. What would this amount to, towards being a steady rule, a certain transcript of a law that we are under? Did the saying of Aristippus, or Confucius, give it an authority? Was Zeno a law-giver to mankind? If not, what he or any other philosopher delivered, was but a saying of his. Mankind might hearken to it or reject it, as they pleased, or as it suited their interest, passions, principles or humours: they were under no obligation; the opinion of this or that philosopher, was of no authority: and if it were, you must take all he said under the same character. All his dictates must go for law, certain and true, or none of them. And then, if you will take any of the moral sayings of Epicurus (many whereof Seneca quotes, with esteem and approbation) for precepts of the law of nature, you must take all the rest of his doctrine for such too, or else his authority ceases: and so no more is to be received from him, or any of the sages of old, for parts of the law of Nature, as carrying with it an obligation to be obeyed, but what they prove to be so. But such a body of Ethics, proved to be the law of nature, from principles of reason, and reaching all the duties of life, I think nobody will say the world had before Our Saviour's time. 'Tis not enough, that there were up and down scattered sayings of wise men, conformable to right reason. The law of nature, was the law of convenience too; and 'tis no wonder that those men of parts, and

studious of virtue (who had occasion to think on any particular part of it), should by meditation light on the right, even from the observable convenience and beauty of it, without making out its obligation from the true principles of the law of nature, and foundations of morality. But these incoherent apophthegms of philosophers, and wise men, however excellent in themselves, and well intended by them, could never make a morality, whereof the world could be convinced; could never rise to the force of a law that mankind could with certainty depend on. Whatsoever should thus be universally useful, as a standard to which men should conform their manners, must have its authority either from reason or revelation. 'Tis not every writer of morals, or compiler of it from others, that can thereby be erected into a law-giver to mankind; and a dictator of rules, which are therefore valid, because they are to be found in his books, under the authority of this or that philosopher. He that any one will pretend to set up in this kind, and have his rules pass for authentic directions, must shew, that either he builds his doctrine upon principles of reason, self-evident in themselves, and that he deduces all the parts of it from thence, by clear and evident demonstration; or, must shew his commission from heaven, that he comes with authority from God, to deliver his will and commands to the world. In the former way, nobody that I know, before Our Saviour's time, ever did, or went about to give us a morality. 'Tis true, there is a law of nature: but who is there that ever did, or undertook to give it us all entire, as a law; no more nor no less, than what was contained in, and had the obligation of that law? Who, ever made out all the parts of it, put them together, and shewed the world their obligation? Where was there any such code, that mankind might have recourse to, as their unerring rule, before Our Saviour's time? If there was not, 'tis plain, there was need of one to give us such a morality; such a law, which might be the sure guide of those who had a desire to go right: and, if they had a mind, need not mistake their duty; but might be certain when they had performed, when failed in it. Such a law of morality, Jesus Christ hath given us in the New Testament; but by the latter of these ways, by revelation. We have from him a full and sufficient rule for our direction, and conformable to that of reason. But the truth and obligation of its precepts, have their force, and are put past doubt to us, by the evidence of his mission. He was sent by God: His miracles shew it; and the authority of God in his precepts cannot be questioned. Here morality has a sure standard, that revelation vouches, and reason cannot gainsay, nor question; but both together witness to come from God the great law-maker. And such an one as this out of the New Testament, I think the world never had, nor can any one say is any where else to be found. Let me ask any one, who is forward to think that the doctrine of morality was full and clear in the world, at Our Saviour's birth; whether would he have directed Brutus and Cassius (both men of parts and virtue, the one whereof believed, and the other disbelieved a future being), to be satisfied in the rules and obligations of all the parts of their duties; if they should have asked him where they might find the law, they were to live by, and by which they should be charged or acquitted, as guilty or innocent? If to the sayings of the wise, and the declarations of philosophers, he sends them into a wild wood of uncertainty, to an endless maze, from which they should never get out: if to the religions of the world, yet worse: and if to their own reason, he refers them to that which had some light and certainty; but yet had hitherto failed all mankind in a perfect rule; and we see, resolved not the doubts that had risen amongst the studious and thinking philosophers; nor had yet been able to convince the civilized parts of the world, that they had not given, nor could, without a crime, take away, the lives of their children, by exposing them.

243. If any one shall think to excuse human nature, by laying blame on men's negligence, that they did not carry morality to an higher pitch; and make it out entire in every part, with that clearness of demonstration which some think it capable of; he helps not the matter. Be the cause what it will, Our Saviour found mankind under a corruption of manners and principles, which ages after ages had prevailed, and must be confessed was not in a way or tendency to be mended. The rules of morality were, in different countries and sects, different. And natural reason no where had, nor was like to cure the defects and errors in them. Those just measures of right and wrong, which necessity had any where introduced, the civil laws prescribed, or philosophy recommended, stood not on their true foundations. They were looked on as bonds of society, and conveniences of common life, and laudable practices. But where was it that their obligation was thoroughly known and allowed, and they received as precepts of a law, of the highest law, the law of nature? That could not be, without a clear

knowledge and acknowledgment of the law-maker, and the great rewards and punishments, for those that would or would not obey him. But the religion of the heathens, as was before observed, little concerned itself in their morals. The priests that delivered the oracles of heaven, and pretended to speak from the God, spoke little of virtue and a good life. And on the other side, the philosophers who spoke from reason, made not much mention of the deity, in their ethics. They depended on reason and her oracles, which contain nothing but truth: but yet some parts of that truth lie too deep for our natural powers easily to reach, and make plain and visible to mankind, without some light from above to direct them. When truths are once known to us, though by tradition, we are apt to be favourable to our own parts, and ascribe to our own understandings the discovery of what, in reality, we borrowed from others; or, at least, finding we can prove what at first we learnt from others, we are forward to conclude it an obvious truth, which, if we had sought, we could not have missed. Nothing seems hard to our understandings, that is once known; and because what we see, we see with our own eyes, we are apt to overlook or forget the help we had from others, who shewed it us, and first made us see it, as if we were not at all beholden to them for those truths they opened the way to, and led us into; for knowledge being only of truths that are perceived to be so, we are favourable enough to our own faculties to conclude, that they, of their own strength, would have attained those discoveries, without any foreign assistance; and that we know those truths by the strength and native light of our own minds, as they did from whom we received them by theirs, only they had the luck to be before us. Thus the whole stock of human knowledge is claimed by every one, as his private possession, as soon as he (profiting by others' discoveries) has got it into his own mind: and so it is; but not properly by his own single industry, nor of his own acquisition. He studies, 'tis true, and takes pains to make a progress in what others have delivered; but their pains were of another sort, who first brought those truths to light, which he afterwards derives from them. He that travels the roads now, applauds his own strength and legs, that have carried him so far in such a scantling of time, and ascribes all to his own vigour, little considering how much he owes to their pains, who cleared the woods, drained the bogs, built the bridges, and made the ways passable; without which he might have toiled much with little progress. A great many things which we have been bred up in the belief of, from our cradles, and are notions grown familiar (and, as it were, natural to us, under the gospel), we take for unquestionable obvious truths, and easily demonstrable; without considering how long we might have been in doubt or ignorance of them, had revelation been silent. And many are beholden to revelation, who do not acknowledge it. 'Tis no diminishing to revelation, that reason gives its suffrage too, to the truths revelation has discovered. But 'tis our mistake to think, that because reason confirms them to us, we had the first certain knowledge of them from thence, and in that clear evidence we now possess them. The contrary is manifest, in the defective morality of the Gentiles before Our Saviour's time, and the want of reformation in the principles and measures of it, as well as practice. Philosophy seemed to have spent its strength, and done its utmost; or if it should have gone farther, as we see it did not, and from undeniable principles given us ethics in a science like mathematics, in every part demonstrable, this yet would not have been so effectual to man in this imperfect state, nor proper for the cure. The greatest part of mankind want leisure or capacity for demonstration, nor can carry a train of proofs, which in that way they must always depend upon for conviction, and cannot be required to assent to till they see the demonstration. Wherever they stick, the teachers are always put upon proof, and must clear the doubt, by a thread of coherent deductions from the first principle, how long, or how intricate soever that be. And you may as soon hope to have all the day-labourers and tradesmen, the spinsters and dairy-maids, perfect mathematicians, as to have them perfect in ethics this way: hearing plain commands, is the sure and only course to bring them to obedience and practice. The greatest part cannot know, and therefore they must believe. And I ask, whether one coming from heaven in the power of God, in full and clear evidence and demonstration of miracles, giving plain and direct rules of morality and obedience, be not likelier to enlighten the bulk of mankind, and set them right in their duties, and bring them to do them, than by reasoning with them from general notions and principles of human reason? And were all the duties of human life clearly demonstrated, yet I conclude, when well considered, that method of teaching men their duties, would be thought proper only for a few, who had much leisure, improved understandings, and were used to abstract reasonings: but the instruction of the people were best still to be left to the precepts and principles of the gospel. The healing of the sick, the restoring sight to the blind by a word, the raising, and being raised from the dead, are matters of fact, which they can without difficulty conceive; and that he who does such things, must do them by the assistance of a divine power. These things lie level to the ordinariest apprehension; he that can distinguish between sick and well, lame and sound, dead and alive, is capable of this doctrine. To one who is once persuaded that Jesus Christ was sent by God to be a King, and a Saviour of those who do believe in him, all his commands become principles; there needs no other proof for the truth of what he says, but that he said it: and then there needs no more but to read the inspired books to be instructed; all the duties of morality lie there clear and plain, and easy to be understood. And here I appeal, whether this be not the surest, the safest, and most effectual way of teaching; especially if we add this farther consideration, that as it suits the lowest capacities of reasonable creatures, so it reaches and satisfies, nay, enlightens the highest. The most elevated understandings cannot but submit to the authority of this doctrine as divine; which coming from the mouths of a company of illiterate men, hath not only the attestation of miracles, but reason to confirm it, since they delivered no precepts, but such, as though reason of itself had not clearly made out, yet it could not but assent to when thus discovered, and think itself indebted for the discovery. The credit and authority Our Saviour and his apostles had over the minds of men, by the miracles they did, tempted them not to mix (as we find in that of all the sects of philosophers, and other religions) any conceits, any wrong rules, any thing tending to their own by-interest, or that of a party, in their morality: no tang of prepossession or fancy; no footsteps of pride or vanity; no touch of ostentation or ambition appears to have a hand in it. It is all pure, all sincere; nothing too much, nothing wanting; but such a complete rule of life, as the wisest men must acknowledge, tends entirely to the good of mankind, and that all would be happy, if all would practise it.

244. 3. The outward forms of worshipping the Deity, wanted a reformation. Stately buildings, costly ornaments, peculiar and uncouth habits, and a numerous huddle of pompous, fantastical, cumbersome ceremonies, every where attended divine worship. This, as it had the peculiar name, so it was thought the principal part, if not the whole of

religion; nor could this possibly be amended whilst the Jewish ritual stood, and there was so much of it mixed with the worship of the true God. To this also Our Saviour, with the knowledge of the infinite, invisible, supreme Spirit, brought a remedy, in a plain, spiritual, and suitable worship. Jesus says to the Woman of Samaria, "The hour cometh, when ye shall neither in this mountain, nor yet at Jerusalem, worship the Father: but the true worshippers, shall worship the Father both in spirit and in truth; for the Father seeketh such to worship." To be worshipped in spirit and in truth, with application of mind and sincerity of heart, was what God henceforth only required. Magnificent temples, and confinement to certain places, were now no longer necessary for his worship, which by a pure heart might be performed any where. The splendour and distinction of habits, and pomp of ceremonies, and all outside performances, might now be spared. God, who was a Spirit, and made known to be so, required none of those, but the spirit only; and that in public assemblies (where some actions must lie open to the view of the world), all that could appear and be seen, should be done decently, and in order, and to edification. Decency, order, and edification, were to regulate all their public acts of worship; and beyond what these required, the outward appearance (which was of little value in the eyes of God) was not to go. Having shut out indecency and confusion out of their assemblies, they need not be solicitous about useless ceremonies. Praises and prayer, humbly offered up to the Deity, was the worship he now demanded; and in these every one was to look after his own heart, and to know that it was that alone which God had regard to, and accepted.

245. 4. Another great advantage received by Our Saviour, is the great encouragement he brought to a virtuous and pious life: great enough to surmount the difficulties and obstacles that lie in the way to it, and reward the pains and hardships of those who stuck firm to their duties, and suffered for the testimony of a good conscience. The portion of the righteous has been in all ages taken notice of to be pretty scanty in this world: virtue and prosperity do not often accompany one another, and therefore virtue seldom had many followers: and 'tis no wonder she prevailed not much in a state, where the inconveniencies that attended her were visible, and at hand, and the rewards doubtful, and at a distance. Mankind, who are and must be allowed to pursue their happiness, nay, cannot be hindered, could not but think themselves

excused from a strict observation of rules, which appeared so little to consist with their chief end, happiness, whilst they kept them from the enjoyments of this life; and they had little evidence and security of another. 'Tis true, they might have argued the other way, and concluded, that, because the good were most of them ill-treated here, there was another place where they should meet with better usage: but 'tis plain they did not. Their thoughts of another life were, at best, obscure; and their expectations uncertain. Of Manes, and ghosts, and the shades of departed men, there was some talk; but little certain, and less minded. They had the names of Styx and Acheron: of Elysian fields, and seats of the blessed: but they had them generally from their poets, mixed with their fables, and so they looked more like the inventions of wit, and ornaments of poetry, than the serious persuasions of the grave and the sober. They came to them bundled up amongst their tales; and for tales they took them. And that which rendered them more suspected, and less useful to virtue, was, that the philosophers seldom set on their rules on men's minds and practices, by consideration of another life. The chief of their arguments were from the excellency of virtue; and the highest they generally went, was the exalting of human nature, whose perfection lay in virtue. And if the priest at any time talked of the ghosts below, and a life after this, it was only to keep men to their superstitious and idolatrous rites, whereby the use of this doctrine was lost to the credulous multitude, and its belief to the quicker sighted, who suspected it presently of priest-craft. Before Our Saviour's time, the doctrine of a future state, though it were not wholly hid, yet it was not clearly known in the world. 'Twas an imperfect view of reason; or, perhaps, the decayed remains of an ancient tradition, which rather seemed to float on men's fancies, than sink deep into their hearts. It was something, they knew not what, between being and not being. Something in man they imagined might escape the grave; but a perfect complete life of an eternal duration, after this, was what entered little into their thoughts, and less into their persuasions. And they were so far from being clear herein, that we see no nation of the world publicly professed it, and built upon it; no religion taught it; and 'twas no where made an article of faith, and principle of religion till Jesus Christ came: of whom it is truly said, that he at his appearing "brought life and immortality to light." And that not only in the clear revelation of it, and in instances shewn of men raised from the dead, but he has given us an unquestionable assurance and pledge of it, in his own resurrection and ascension into heaven. How hath this one truth changed the nature of things in the world? And given the advantage to piety over all that could tempt or deter men from it. The philosophers, indeed, shewed the beauty of virtue: they set her off so as drew men's eyes and approbation to her; but leaving her unendowed, very few were willing to espouse her. The generality could not refuse her their esteem and commendation, but still turned their backs on her, and forsook her, as a match not for their turn. But now there being put into the scales, on her side, "an exceeding and immortal weight of glory," interest is come about to her; and virtue now is visibly the most enriching purchase, and by much the best bargain. That she is the perfection and excellency of our nature; that she is herself a reward, and will recommend our names to future ages, is not all that can now be said for her. 'Tis not strange that the learned heathens satisfied not many with such airy commendations. It has another relish and efficacy to persuade men, that if they live well here, they shall be happy hereafter. Open their eyes upon the endless unspeakable joys of another life; and their hearts will find something solid and powerful to move them. The view of heaven and hell will cast a slight upon the short pleasures and pains of this present state, and give attractions and encouragements to virtue, which reason and interest, and the care of ourselves, cannot but allow and prefer. Upon this foundation, and upon this only, morality stands firm, and may defy all competition. This makes it more than a name, a substantial good, worth all our aims and endeavours; and thus the gospel of Jesus Christ has delivered it to us.

246. 5. To these I must add one advantage more by Jesus Christ, and that is the promise of assistance. If we do what we can, he will give us his Spirit to help us to do what, and how we should. 'Twill be idle for us, who know not how our own spirits move and act us, to ask in what manner the Spirit of God shall work upon us. The wisdom that accompanies that Spirit, knows better than we how we are made, and how to work upon us. If a wise man knows how to prevail on his child, to bring him to what he desires, can we suspect, that the Spirit and wisdom of God should fail in it, though we perceive or comprehend not the ways of his operation? Christ has promised it, who is faithful and just, and we cannot doubt of the performance. 'Tis not requisite on this occasion for the enhancing of this benefit, to enlarge

on the frailty of minds, and weakness of our constitutions; how liable to mistakes, how apt to go astray, and how easily to be turned out of the paths of virtue. If any one needs go beyond himself, and the testimony of his own conscience in this point; if he feels not his own errors and passions always tempting him, and often prevailing, against the strict rules of his duty, he need but look abroad into any age of the world to be convinced. To a man under the difficulties of his nature, beset with temptations, and hedged in with prevailing custom; 'tis no small encouragement to set himself seriously on the courses of virtue, and practice of true religion, that he is from a sure hand, and an almighty arm, promised assistance to support and carry him through.

247. There remains yet something to be said to those, who will be ready to object, "If the belief of Jesus of Nazareth to be the Messiah, together with those concomitant articles of his resurrection, rule and coming again to judge the world, be all the faith required, as necessary to justification, to what purpose were the epistles written; I say, if the belief of those many doctrines contained in them, be not also necessary to salvation; and if what is there delivered, a Christian may believe or disbelieve, and yet nevertheless, be a member of Christ's Church, and one of the faithful?"

248. To this, I answer, That the epistles were written upon several occasions: and he that will read them as he ought, must observe what 'tis in them, is principally aimed at; find what is the argument in hand, and how managed; if he will understand them right, and profit by them. The observing of this will best help us to the true meaning and mind of the writer; for that is the truth which is to be received and believed, and not scattered sentences in a Scripture-language accommodated to our notions and prejudices. We must look into the drift of the discourse, observe the coherence and connexion of the parts, and see how it is consistent with itself, and other parts of Scripture, if we will conceive it right. We must not cull out, as best suits our system, here and there a period or a verse, as if they were all distinct and independent aphorisms; and make these the fundamental articles of the Christian faith, and necessary to salvation, unless God has made them so. There be many truths in the Bible, which a good Christian may be wholly ignorant of, and so not believe, which, perhaps, some lay great stress on, and call fundamental articles, because they are the distinguishing points of their communion. The epistles, most of them,

carry on a thread of argument, which in the style they are writ, cannot everywhere be observed without great attention. And to consider the texts, as they stand and bear a part in that, is to view them in their due light, and the way to get the true sense of them. They were writ to those who were in the faith, and true Christians already; and so could not be designed to teach them the fundamental articles and points necessary to salvation. The Epistle to the Romans was writ to all that were "at Rome, beloved of God, called to be the Saints", whose faith was "spoken of through the world", Ch. i. 7, 8. To whom St. Paul's first Epistle to the Corinthians was, he shews, Ch. i. 2, 4, etc., "Unto the church of God which is at Corinth, to them that are sanctified in Christ Jesus, called to be saints; with all them that in every place call upon the name of Jesus Christ our Lord, both theirs and ours. I thank my God always on your behalf, for the grace of God which is given you by Jesus Christ; that in every thing ye are enriched by him in all utterance, and in all knowledge: even as the testimony of Christ was confirmed in you. So that ye come behind in no gift; waiting for the coming of the Lord Jesus Christ." And so likewise the second was, "To the church of God at Corinth, with all the saints in Achaia", Ch. i. 1. His next is to the churches of Galatia. That to the Ephesians was, "To the saints that were at Ephesus, and to the faithful in Christ Jesus". So likewise, "To the saints and faithful brethren in Christ at Colosse", who had faith in Christ Jesus, and love to the saints. "To the church of the Thessalonians." "To Timothy" his "son in the faith". "To Titus" his "own son after the common faith". "To Philemon" his "dearly beloved, and fellow labourer". And the author to the Hebrews, calls those he writes to, "Holy brethren, partakers of the heavenly calling", Ch. iii. 1. From whence it is evident, that all those whom St. Paul wrote to, were brethren, saints, faithful in the Church, and so Christians already, and therefore wanted not the fundamental articles of the Christian religion; without a belief of which they could not be saved: nor can it be supposed, that the sending of such fundamentals was the reason of the apostle's writing to any of them. To such also St. Peter writes, as is plain from the first chapter of each of his epistles. Nor is it hard to observe the like in St. James and St. John's epistles. And St. Jude directs his thus: "To them that are sanctified by God the Father, and preserved in Jesus Christ, and called." The epistles therefore being all written to those who were already believers and

Christians, the occasion and end of writing them, could not be to instruct them in that which was necessary to make them Christians. This 'tis plain they knew and believed already; or else they could not have been Christians and believers. And they were writ upon particular occasions; and without those occasions had not been writ, and so cannot be thought necessary to salvation; though they resolving doubts, and reforming mistakes, are of great advantage to our knowledge and practice. I do not deny, but the great doctrines of the Christian faith are dropped here and there, and scattered up and down in most of them. But 'tis not in the epistles we are to learn what are the fundamental articles of faith, where they are promiscuously, and without distinction mixed with other truths in discourses that were (though for edification indeed, yet) only occasional. We shall find and discern those great and necessary points best in the preaching of Our Saviour and the apostles, to those who were yet strangers, and ignorant of the faith, to bring them in, and convert them to it. And what that was, we have seen already out of the history of the evangelists, and the Acts; where they are plainly laid down, so that nobody can mistake them. The epistles to particular churches, besides the main argument of each of them (which was some present concernment of that particular church to which they severally were addressed) do in many places explain the fundamentals of the Christian religion; and that wisely, by proper accommodations to the apprehensions of those they were writ to, the better to make them imbibe the Christian doctrine, and the more easily to comprehend the method, reasons, and grounds of the great work of salvation. Thus we see in the epistle to the Romans, adoption (a custom well known amongst those of Rome) is much made use of, to explain to them the grace and favour of God, in giving them eternal life; to help them to conceive how they became the children of God, and to assure them of a share in the kingdom of heaven, as heirs to an inheritance. Whereas the setting out, and confirming the Christian faith to the Hebrews, in the epistle to them, is by allusions and arguments, from the ceremonies, sacrifices, and oeconomy of the Jews, and reference to the records of the Old Testament. And as for the general epistles, they, we may see, regard the state and exigencies, and some peculiarities of those times. These holy writers, inspired from above, writ nothing but truth, and in most places very weighty truths to us now; for the expounding, clearing, and confirming of the Christian doctrine, and establishing those in it who had embraced it. But yet every sentence of theirs must not be taken up and looked on as a fundamental article necessary to salvation; without an explicit belief whereof, nobody could be a member of Christ's church here, nor be admitted into his eternal kingdom hereafter. If all, or most of the truths declared in the epistles, were to be received and believed as fundamental articles, what then became of those Christians who were fallen asleep (as St. Paul witnesses in his first to the Corinthians, many were) before these things in the epistles were revealed to them? Most of the epistles not being written till above twenty years after Our Saviour's ascension, and some after thirty.

249. But further, therefore, to those who will be ready to say, "May those truths delivered in the epistles, which are not contained in the preaching of Our Saviour and his apostles, and are therefore, by this account, not necessary to salvation, be believed or disbelieved without any danger? May a Christian safely question or doubt of them?"

250. To this I answer, That the law of faith, being a covenant of free grace, God alone can appoint what shall be necessarily believed by every one whom he will justify. What is the faith which he will accept and account for righteousness, depends wholly on his good pleasure; for 'tis of grace, and not of right, that this faith is accepted. And therefore he alone can set the measures of it; and what he has so appointed and declared, is alone necessary. Nobody can add to these fundamental articles of faith, nor make any other necessary, but what God himself hath made and declared to be so. And what these are, which God requires of those who will enter into, and receive the benefits of the new covenant, has already been shewn. An explicit belief of these is absolutely required, of all those, to whom the gospel of Jesus Christ is preached, and salvation through his Name proposed.

251. The other parts of divine revelation are objects of faith, and are so to be received. They are truths, whereof no one can be rejected; none that is once known to be such, may or ought to be disbelieved; for to acknowledge any proposition to be of divine revelation and authority, and yet to deny or disbelieve it, is to offend against this fundamental article, and ground of faith, that God is true. But yet a great many of the truths revealed in the gospel, every one does, and must confess, a man may be ignorant of; nay, disbelieve, without

danger to his salvation: as is evident in those, who, allowing the authority, differ in the interpretation and meaning of several texts of Scripture, not thought fundamental: in all which, 'tis plain, the contending parties on one side or the other, are ignorant of, nay, disbelieve the truths delivered in holy writ; unless contrarieties and contradictions can be contained in the same words, and divine revelation can mean contrary to itself.

252. Though all divine revelation requires the obedience of faith; yet every truth of inspired scriptures is not one of those, that by the law of faith is required to be explicitly believed to justification. What those are, we have seen by what Our Saviour and his apostles proposed to, and required in those whom they converted to the faith. Those are fundamentals, which 'tis not enough not to disbelieve, every one is required actually to assent to them. But any other proposition contained in the Scripture, which God has not thus made a necessary part of the law of faith (without an actual assent to which he will not allow any one to be a believer) a man may be ignorant of, without hazarding his salvation by a defect in his faith. He believes all that God has made necessary for him to believe and assent to; and as for the rest of divine truths, there is nothing more required of him, but that he receive all the parts of divine revelation, with a docility and disposition prepared to embrace, and assent to all truths coming from God; and submit his mind to whatsoever shall appear to him to bear that character. Where he, upon fair endeavours understands it not, how can he avoid being ignorant? And where he cannot put several texts, and make them consist together, what remedy? He must either interpret one by the other, or suspend his opinion. He that thinks that more is, or can be required, of poor frail man in matters of faith, will do well to consider what absurdities he will run into. God, out of the infiniteness of his mercy, has dealt with man as a compassionate and tender Father. He gave him reason, and with it a law, that could not be otherwise than what reason should dictate, unless we should think, that a reasonable creature, should have an unreasonable law. But considering the frailty of man, apt to run into corruption and misery, he promised a deliverer, whom in his good time he sent; and then declared to all mankind, that whoever would believe him to be the Saviour promised, and take him now raised from the dead, and constituted the Lord and Judge of all men, to be their King and Ruler, should be saved. This is a plain

intelligible proposition; and the all-merciful God seems herein to have consulted the poor of this world, and the bulk of mankind: these are articles that the labouring and illiterate man may comprehend. This is a religion suited to vulgar capacities, and the state of mankind in this world, destined to labour and travail. The writers and wranglers in religion fill it with niceties, and dress it up with notions, which they make necessary and fundamental parts of it; as if there were no way into the Church, but through the Academy or Lycæum. The greatest part of mankind have not leisure for learning and logic, and superfine distinctions of the schools. Where the hand is used to the plough and the spade, the head is seldom elevated to sublime notions, or exercised in mysterious reasonings. 'Tis well if men of that rank (to say nothing of the other sex) can comprehend plain propositions, and a short reasoning about things familiar to their minds, and nearly allied to their daily experience. Go beyond this, and you amaze the greatest part of mankind; and may as well talk Arabic to a poor day labourer, as the notions and language that the books and disputes of religion are filled with, and as soon you will be understood. The dissenting congregations, are supposed by their teachers, to be more accurately instructed in matters of faith, and better to understand the Christian religion, than the vulgar conformists, who are charged with great ignorance; how truly I will not here determine. But I ask them to tell me seriously, whether half their people have leisure to study? Nay, whether one in ten of those who come to their meetings in the country, if they had time to study, do or can understand the controversies at this time so warmly managed amongst them, about justification, the subject of this present treatise? I have talked with some of their teachers, who confess themselves not to understand the difference in debate between them: and yet the points they stand on, are reckoned of so great weight, so material, so fundamental in religion, that they divide communion, and separate upon them. Had God intended that none but the learned scribe, the disputer or wise of this world, should be Christians, or be saved; thus religion should have been prepared for them, filled with speculations and niceties, obscure terms, and abstract notions. But men of that expectation, men furnished with such acquisitions, the apostle tells us, 1 Cor. i, are rather shut out from the simplicity of the gospel, to make way for those poor, ignorant, illiterate, who heard and believed the promises of a deliverer, and believed Jesus to be him; who could conceive a man dead and made alive again, and, believe that he should, at the end of the world, come again, and pass sentence on all men, according to their deeds. That the poor had the gospel preached to them, Christ makes a mark, as well as business, of his mission, Matt. xi. 5. And if the poor had the gospel preached to them, it was, without doubt, such a gospel as the poor could understand, plain and intelligible: and so it was, as we have seen, in the preachings of Christ and his apostles.

A DISCOURSE OF MIRACLES

I. INTRODUCTORY NOTE

As Locke tells us at the end, this *Discourse* was "occasioned by my reading Mr. Fleetwood's[1] Essay on Miracles, and the letter writ to him on that subject. The one of them defining a miracle to be an extraordinary operation performable by God alone: and the other writing of miracles without any definition of a miracle at all."

Here Locke emphasizes that the definition of miracle must inevitably have reference to the observer. To define a miracle by reference to what God alone could know, is pointless; such a definition God alone could apply. On the other hand, the reference to the observer means that a miracle must needs be considered in relation to a wider situation which in the end not only includes the miraculous event as such and the observer, but someone claiming to have a mission from God with the miracle as evidence of that claim. A miracle is no mere wonder; for Locke, it must be a witness to somebody of someone's mission from God. The significance of a miracle is therefore the power of God it exhibits in the totality of a certain situation, and the criteria for a miracle will thus be criteria of such power.

What criteria have we? Here, Locke plainly finds it difficult to go beyond the kind of consideration he has given us in the *Essay* (Bk. IV. Chs. 18 and 19)[2]. No event could be justly called a miracle—however wonderful—if it supported claims "inconsistent with natural religion and the rules of morality"[3]; nor will a miracle characterize a situation confined to trivialities. Rather more positively Locke says that a miracle must testify to truths "relating to the glory of God, and some great concern of men"[4]. But may we not sometimes have to judge

---

[1] This was William Fleetwood (1656–1733) some time Fellow of King's College, Cambridge, and successively Bishop of St. Asaph (1708) and of Ely (1714). He published in 1701 an *Essay on Miracles, in Two Discourses*. This essay contained material which he had collected for the Boyle Lectureship, though ill health prevented him from giving the lectures. To this essay Bishop Hoadly wrote a reply, but Fleetwood, who cared little for controversy, never took the matter further.

[2] and to which some reference is made above pp. 11–12.

[3] see below p. 84 (1).   [4] see below p. 84 (3).

between two miracles indistinguishable by such general criteria, whereupon we have to ask which displays the "greater power"? Here Locke is face to face with an epistemological difficulty he never really solved. No doubt he would like to think that a criterion of greater power could be unambiguously given in terms of ideas of sensation; but his attempt to give criteria of greater power wholly in terms of such ideas (so that one "power" was greater than another if the serpents produced by the one devoured the serpents produced by the other) shows how unsatisfactory this is, and we are reminded of all his difficulties in the *Essay* over this concept of power. We are reminded of Locke's confession (*Essay*, Bk. II, Ch. 21, para. 4) that "we have, from the observation of the operations of bodies by our senses, but a very imperfect, obscure idea of active power", which comes rather "from reflection on what passes in ourselves". Is our notion of power, then, given by an intuition such as that which occurs when we bring together in ourselves ideas of reflection?

If so, miraculous power, like our own activity, is never adequately portrayed in terms of ideas of sensation. Belief in miracle is both as reasonable and problematical as our belief in other people's activity. No observable criteria will ever be adequate to either, as no observable criteria gives to ourselves or others an adequate account of our own activity. All we can do in the case of miracle is to have as many such criteria as possible; to employ certain negative tests such as Locke mentions above; all the time recognizing that a miracle stands or falls by the power of God it displays. So we must realize that in the end we are dealing with something which inevitably goes beyond any and all ideas of sensation and criteria relating thereto, being as "mysterious" as is knowledge of myself to others.

2. TEXT

A DISCOURSE OF MIRACLES

To discourse of miracles without defining what one means by the word miracle, is to make a shew, but in effect to talk of nothing.

A miracle then I take to be a sensible operation, which, being above the comprehension of the spectator, and in his opinion contrary to the established course of nature, is taken by him to be divine.

He that is present at the fact, is a spectator. He that believes the history of the facts, puts himself in the place of a spectator.

This definition, 'tis probable, will not escape these two exceptions.

1. That hereby what is a miracle is made very uncertain; for it depending on the opinion of the spectator, that will be a miracle to one which will not be so to another.

In answer to which, it is enough to say, that this objection is of no force, but in the mouth of one who can produce a definition of a miracle not liable to the same exception, which I think not easy to do; for it being agreed, that a miracle must be that which surpasses the force of nature in the established, steady laws of causes and effects, nothing can be taken to be a miracle but what is judged to exceed those laws. Now every one being able to judge of those laws only by his own acquaintance with Nature; and notions of its force (which are different in different men) it is unavoidable that that should be a miracle to one, which is not so to another.

2. Another objection to this definition, will be, that the notion of a miracle thus enlarged, may come sometimes to take in operations that have nothing extraordinary or supernatural in them, and thereby invalidate the use of miracles for the attesting of divine revelation.

To which I answer, not at all, if the testimony which divine revelation receives from miracles be rightly considered.

To know that any revelation is from God, it is necessary to know that the messenger that delivers it is sent from God, and that cannot be known but by some credential given him by God himself. Let us see then whether miracles, in my sense, be not such credentials, and will not infallibly direct us right in the search of divine revelation.

It is to be considered, that divine revelation receives testimony from no other miracles, but such as are wrought to witness his mission from God who delivers the revelation. All other miracles that are done in the world, how many or great soever, revelation is not concerned in. Cases wherein there has been, or can be need of miracles for the confirmation of revelation, are fewer than perhaps is imagined. The heathen world, amidst an infinite and uncertain jumble of deities, fables and worships, had no room for a divine attestation of any one against the rest. Those owners of many gods were at liberty in their worship; and no one of their divinities pretending to be the one only true God, no one of them could be supposed in the pagan scheme to make use of miracles to establish his worship alone, or to abolish that of the other; much less was there any use of miracles to confirm any articles of faith, since no one of them had any such to propose as necessary to be believed by their votaries. And therefore I do not remember any miracles recorded in the Greek or Roman writers, as done to confirm any one's mission or doctrine. Conformable hereunto we find St. Paul, 1 Cor. i. 22, takes notice that the Jews ('tis true) required miracles, but as for the Greeks they looked after something else; they knew no need or use there was of miracles to recommend any religion to them. And indeed it is an astonishing mark how far the God of this world had blinded men's minds, if we consider that the Gentile world received and stuck to a religion, which, not being derived from reason, had no sure foundation in revelation. They knew not its original, nor the authors of it, nor seemed concerned to know from whence it came, or by whose authority delivered; and so had no mention or use of miracles for its confirmation. For though there were here and there some pretences to revelation, yet there were not so much as pretences to miracles that attested it.

If we will direct our thoughts by what has been, we must conclude that miracles, as the credentials of a messenger delivering a divine religion, have no place but upon a supposition of one only true God; and that it is so in the nature of the thing, and cannot be otherwise, I think will be made appear in the sequel of this discourse. Of such who have come in the name of the one only true God, professing to bring a law from him, we have in history a clear account but of three, viz. Moses, Jesus and Mahomet. For what the Persees say of their Zoroaster, or the Indians of their Brama (not to mention all the wild stories of the religions farther east) is so obscure, or so manifestly fabulous, that no account can be made of it. Now of the three before-mentioned, Mahomet having none to produce, pretends to no miracles for the vouching of his mission; so that the only revelations that come attested by miracles, being only those of Moses and Christ, and they confirming each other, the business of miracles, as it stands really in matter of fact, has no manner of difficulty in it; and I think the most scrupulous or sceptical cannot from miracles raise the least doubt against the divine revelation of the gospel.

But since the speculative and learned will be putting of cases which never were, and it may be presumed never will be; since scholars and disputants will be raising of questions where there are none, and enter upon debates whereof there is no need; I crave leave to say, that he who comes with a message from God to be delivered to the world, cannot be refused belief if he vouches his mission by a miracle, because his credentials have a right to it. For every rational thinking man must conclude as Nicodemus did, "We know that thou art a teacher come from God, for no man can do these signs which thou doest, except God be with him."

For example, Jesus of Nazareth professes himself sent from God: He with a word calms a tempest at sea. This one looks on as a miracle, and consequently cannot but receive his doctrine. Another thinks this might be the effect of chance, or skill in the weather and no miracle, and so stands out; but afterwards seeing him walk on the sea, owns that for a miracle and believes; which yet upon another has not that force, who suspects it may possibly be done by the assistance of a spirit. But yet the same person, seeing afterwards Our Saviour cure an inveterate palsy by a word, admits that for a miracle, and becomes a convert. Another overlooking it in this instance, afterwards finds a miracle in his giving sight to one born blind, or in raising the dead, or his raising himself from the dead, and so receives his doctrine as a revelation coming from God. By all which it is plain, that where the miracle is admitted, the doctrine cannot be rejected; it comes with the assurance of a divine attestation to him that allows the miracle, and he cannot question its truth.

The next thing then is, what shall be a sufficient inducement to take any extraordinary operation to be a miracle, i.e. wrought by God himself for the attestation of a revelation from him?

And to this I answer, the carrying with it the marks of a greater power than appears in opposition to it. For:

1. First, this removes the main difficulty where it presses hardest, and clears the matter from doubt, when extraordinary and supernatural operations are brought to support opposite missions, about which methinks more dust has been raised by men of leisure than so plain a matter needed. For since God's power is paramount to all, and no opposition can be made against him with an equal force to his; and since his honour and goodness can never be supposed to suffer his messenger and his truth to be born down by the appearance of a greater power on the side of an impostor, and in favour of a lie;

wherever there is an opposition, and two pretending to be sent from heaven clash, the signs, which carry with them the evident marks of a greater power, will always be a certain and unquestionable evidence, that the truth and divine mission are on that side on which they appear. For though the discovery, how the lying wonders are or can be produced, be beyond the capacity of the ignorant, and often beyond the conception of the most knowing spectator, who is therefore forced to allow them in his apprehension to be above the force of natural causes and effects; yet he cannot but know they are not seals set by God to his truth for the attesting of it, since they are opposed by miracles that carry the evident marks of a greater and superior power, and therefore they cannot at all shake the authority of one so supported. God can never be thought to suffer that a lie, set up in opposition to a truth coming from him, should be backed with a greater power than he will shew for the confirmation and propagation of a doctrine which he has revealed, to the end it might be believed. The producing of serpents, blood and frogs, by the Egyptian sorcerers and by Moses, could not to the spectators but appear equally miraculous, which of the pretenders then had their mission from God: and the truth on their side could not have been determined if the matter had rested there. But when Moses's serpent ate up theirs, when he produced lice which they could not, the decision was easy. 'Twas plain Jannes and Jambres acted by an inferior power, and their operations, how marvellous and extraordinary soever, could not in the least bring in question Moses's mission; that stood the firmer for this opposition, and remained the more unquestionable after this, than if no such signs had been brought against it.

So likewise the number, variety and greatness of the miracles, wrought for the confirmation of the doctrine delivered by Jesus Christ, carry with them such strong marks of an extraordinary divine power, that the truth of his mission will stand firm and unquestionable, till any one rising up in opposition to him shall do greater miracles than he and his apostles did. For any thing less will not be of weight to turn the scales in the opinion of any one, whether of an inferior or more exalted understanding. This is one of those palpable truths and trials, of which all mankind are judges; and there needs no assistance of learning, no deep thought to come to a certainty in it. Such care has God taken that no pretended revelation should stand in competition with what is truly divine, that we need but open our eyes to see and be sure which came from him. The marks of his over-ruling power accompany it; and therefore to this day we find, that wherever the gospel comes, it prevails to the beating down the strongholds of Satan, and the dislodging the Prince of the Power of Darkness, driving him away with all his living wonders; which is a standing miracle, carrying with it the testimony of superiority.

What is the uttermost power of natural agents or created beings, men of the greatest reach cannot discover; but that it is not equal to God's omnipotency is obvious to everyone's understanding; so that the superior power is an easy, as well as sure guide to divine revelation, attested by miracles where they are brought as credentials to an embassy from God.

And thus upon the same grounds of superiority of power, uncontested revelation will stand too.

For the explaining of which, it may be necessary to premise:

1. That no mission can be looked on to be divine, that delivers any thing derogating from the honour of the one, only, true, invisible God, or inconsistent with natural religion and the rules of morality: because God having discovered to men the unity and majesty of his eternal Godhead, and the truths of natural religion and morality by the light of reason, he cannot be supposed to back the contrary by revelation; for that would be to destroy the evidence and the use of reason, without which men cannot be able to distinguish divine revelation from diabolical imposture.

2. That it cannot be expected that God should send any one into the world on purpose to inform men of things indifferent, and of small moment, or that are knowable by the use of their natural faculties. This would be to lessen the dignity of his majesty in favour of our sloth, and in prejudice to our reason.

3. The only case then wherein a mission of any one from heaven can be reconciled to the high and awful thoughts men ought to have of the deity, must be the revelation of some supernatural truths relating to the glory of God, and some great concern of men. Supernatural operations attesting such a revelation may, with reason, be taken to be miracles, as carrying the marks of a superior and over-ruling power, as long as no revelation accompanied with marks of a greater power appears against it. Such supernatural signs may justly stand good, and

be received for divine, i.e. wrought by a power superior to all, 'till a
mission attested by operations of a greater force shall disprove them:
because it cannot be supposed, God should suffer his prerogative to be
so far usurped by any inferior being, as to permit any creature, depending on him, to set his seals, the marks of his divine authority, to a
mission coming from him. For these supernatural signs being the only
means God is conceived to have to satisfy men as rational creatures of
the certainty of any thing he would reveal, as coming from himself,
can never consent that it should be wrested out of his hands, to serve
the ends and establish the authority of an inferior agent that rivals
him. His power being known to have no equal, always will, and always
may be safely depended on, to shew its superiority in vindicating his
authority, and maintaining every truth that he hath revealed. So that
the marks of a superior power accompanying it, always have been,
and always will be a visible and sure guide to divine revelation; by
which men may conduct themselves in their examining of revealed
religions, and be satisfied which they ought to receive as coming from
God; though they have by no means ability precisely to determine
what it is, or is not above the force of any created being; or what
operations can be performed by none but a divine power, and require
the immediate hand of the Almighty. And therefore we see 'tis by
that Our Saviour measures the great unbelief of the Jews, John xv. 24,
saying, "If I had not done among them the works which no other man
did, they had not had sin, but now have they both seen and hated both
me and my Father"; declaring, that they could not but see the power
and presence of God in those many miracles he did, which were greater
than ever any other man had done. When God sent Moses to the
children of Israel with a message, that now according to his promise he
would redeem them by his hand out of Egypt, and furnished him with
signs and credentials of his mission; it is very remarkable what God
himself says of those signs, Exod. iv. 8, "And it shall come to pass, if
they will not believe thee, nor hearken to the voice of the first sign"
(which was turning his rod into a serpent) "that they will believe, and
the voice of the latter sign" (which was the making his hand leprous
by putting it in his bosom); God further adds, ver. 9, "And it shall
come to pass, if they will not believe also these two signs, neither
hearken unto thy voice, that thou shalt take of the water of the river
and pour upon the dry land: And the water which thou takest out of

the river shall become blood upon the dry land." Which of those operations was or was not above the force of all created beings, will, I suppose, be hard for any man, too hard for a poor brick-maker to determine; and therefore the credit and certain reception of the mission, was annexed to neither of them, but the prevailing of their attestation was heightened by the increase of their number; two supernatural operations shewing more power than one, and three more than two. God allowed that it was natural, that the marks of greater power should have a greater impression on the minds and belief of the spectators. Accordingly the Jews, by this estimate judged of the miracles of Our Saviour, John vii. 31, where we have this account, "and many of the people believed on him, and said when Christ cometh will he do more miracles than these which this man hath done?" This perhaps, as it is the plainest, so it is also the surest way to preserve the testimony of miracles in its due force to all sorts and degrees of people. For miracles being the basis on which divine mission is always established, and consequently that foundation on which the believers of any divine revelation must ultimately bottom their faith, this use of them would be lost, if not to all mankind, yet at least to the simple and illiterate (which is the far greatest part) if miracles be defined to be none but such divine operations as are in themselves beyond the power of all created beings, or at least operations contrary to the fixed and established laws of Nature. For as to the latter of those, what are the fixed and established laws of Nature, philosophers alone, if at least they can pretend to determine. And if they are to be operations performable only by divine power, I doubt whether any man learned or unlearned, can in most cases be able to say of any particular operation, that can fall under his senses, that it is certainly a miracle. Before he can come to that certainty, he must know that no created being has a power to perform it. We know good and bad angels have abilities and excellencies exceedingly beyond all our poor performances or narrow comprehensions. But to define what is the utmost extent of power that any of them has, is a bold undertaking of a man in the dark, that pronounces without seeing, and sets bounds to his narrow cell to things at an infinite distance from his model and comprehension.

Such definitions therefore of miracles, however specious in discourse and theory, fail us when we come to use, and an application of them in particular cases.

These thoughts concerning miracles, were occasioned by my reading Mr. Fleetwood's *Essay on Miracles*, and the letter writ to him on that subject. The one of them defining a miracle to be an extraordinary operation performable by God alone: and the other writing of miracles without any definition of a miracle at all.

A FURTHER NOTE ON MIRACLES

being a Selection from Chapter X of
A Third Letter Concerning Toleration

I. INTRODUCTORY NOTE

It is hardly surprising that Locke, philosopher and man of affairs, with loyalties to both Church and State, growing up in years of civil war, should have been specially concerned about toleration.

In 1685, while in Holland, he addressed the *Epistula de Tolerantia* to Limborch, the Remonstrant Divine. This letter, based on an unpublished work, written almost twenty years earlier, was translated in the same year into English, French and Dutch. In answer to criticisms Locke wrote three subsequent letters (one of which—a fragment—was published posthumously),[1] and it is from *A Third Letter concerning Toleration* that our extract is taken. The four letters of which the first is by far the most important, together constitute the definitive expression of the Whig doctrine of Toleration: and (though we shall not here be further concerned with the point) it is in the first *Letter* that there occurs Locke's famous concept of the Church as a voluntary society:

"A Church . . . I take to be a voluntary society of men, joining themselves together of their own accord, in order to the public worshipping of God, in such a manner as they judge acceptable to him, and effectual to the salvation of their souls."

Returning now to our extract from the *Third Letter*, we must

---

[1] The dates of publication were as follows:
Epistula de Tolerantia (and translations) 1689; *A Second Letter concerning Toleration*, 1690; and *A Third Letter concerning Toleration*, 1692. These last two letters were both signed Philanthropus, and replied respectively to attacks by Jonas Proast who first in 1690 had written *The Argument of the Letter concerning Toleration briefly considered and answered*; and then in 1691 had written *A Third Letter concerning Toleration*. The enumeration is not a little misleading since Proast's *Third Letter* was his first letter and only "third" in relation to Locke's "Second" letter. Indeed afterwards (in 1704) Proast wrote what for him was the second letter on the topic when he published *A Second Letter to the author of the three letters for toleration*. It was this letter to which Locke was drafting a reply when he died, and this fragmentary reply was included in Locke's *Posthumous Works* published in 1706.

remember that Locke's opponent[1] had argued that there was "no reason, from any experiment, to expect that the true religion should be, any way, a gainer by toleration," by the kind of toleration, that is, which merely gave it freedom to be preached. Locke had countered this by pointing to "the prevailing of the gospel, by its own beauty, force and reasonableness in the first ages of Christianity." But, said his opponent, it also had in those days the support of miracles as well, and these provided that compelling power which later the State should and could supply. Locke's opponent was arguing in effect that people can be justly punished by the civil power for failing to embrace the Christian religion, because in this way the civil power is only supplying the same kind of power as in earlier days was given to the Christian religion by its miracles.

For our present purpose we may distinguish in this discussion, two questions:

1. Does the Christian faith need more than "its own beauty, force and reasonableness" if these words are so interpreted as to exclude miracles? Locke would have certainly answered "Yes"; for Locke, the Christian miracles were indispensable. But we must remember how he would have argued for their reasonableness, so that in fact for him the phrases we have quoted would not have been interpreted so as to exclude miracles. Miracles readily witnessed to the "force and reasonableness" of the Christian faith. Which brings us to our second question.

2. Is the power of miracles equivalent to the power of the civil

[1] This opponent was Jonas Proast who took his B.A. from The Queen's College, Oxford, in 1663 and subsequently became Chaplain of All Souls. He died in 1710.

He was notable in his day for the circumstances surrounding his expulsion from All Souls. In 1688 he was expelled by the new Warden, Leopold Finch, for contempt. But Wood tells us that "'twas for not giving his vote for the Warden when he stood to be History Professor and for being medling [sic] and troublesome in the house. When the Warden stood he sent for all the fellows and chaplains to desire their votes and then Mr. Proast told him he was engaged for another." (*The Life and Times of Anthony Wood*, ed. Andrew Clark, Vol. III, p. 263).

Proast appealed to the Archbishop of Canterbury, as Visitor, and ultimately had the Warden's decree reversed. But in 1692 it was said of him that "he will not take possession till he hath the arrears paid for the time that he was ejected" (*ibid.*, p. 404). The Archbishop's order for the restoration is dated 15th March 1694.

It is interesting to reflect that it was in these troublesome years when Proast was very personally concerned with the exercise of authoritative power both for and against him, that he contested Locke's doctrine of Toleration.

State? It was on this question that Locke and his opponent differed. What Locke denied, and what his opponent believed, was that the compelling power of miracles was the same as the compelling power of the State.

It is common ground between Locke and his opponent that more than "preaching and persuasion" may be wanted for a person to become a Christian. There will be need of the grace of God. But, says Locke's opponent, the assistance of "human means" is needed as well, and this is precisely what a miracle supplies. But Locke's view is that miracles for the Christian concern more than "outward . . . and external force". There is, Locke would say, about miracles, something inwardly compelling. The discussion continues, and our extract is taken from Chapter X of the *Third Letter*, which bears for its title: "Of the necessity of force in matters of religion". Here Locke is concerned to argue precisely this point at issue. For him the compelling "power" of miracles is inwardly compelling, and is not a "power" which, comparable to the power of the civil State, can be exhaustively described in terms of objective penalties and punishments. So I would suggest that Locke's view is that miracles, concerning as they do the power of God, will never be tractable in terms of clear and distinct ideas, but are something of which in the last resort we are intuitively aware; something which, in this sense, are mysterious. His *Discourse of Miracles* makes, as I have tried to show,[2] the same point.

2. TEXT

A THIRD LETTER CONCERNING TOLERATION

Selections from Chapter X

The question between us here, is, whether the Christian religion did not prevail in the first ages of the Church by its own beauty, force and reasonableness, without the assistance of force? I say, it did, and therefore external force is not necessary. To this you reply, "that it cannot prevail, by its own light, and strength, without the assistance either of miracles, or of authority; and therefore the Christian religion not being still accompanied with miracles, force is now necessary". So that, to make your equivalent, of miracles, correspond with your necessary

[2] See pp. 78–79 above.

means of force, you seem to require an actual application of miracles, or of force, to prevail with men to receive the gospel, i.e. men could not be prevailed with, to receive the gospel, without actually seeing of miracles. For, when you tell us, that "you are sure, I cannot say the Christian religion is still accompanied with miracles, as it was, at its first planting"; I hope you do not mean that the gospel is not still accompanied with an undoubted testimony, that miracles were done, by the first publishers of it, which was as much of miracles, as I suppose the greatest part of those had, with whom the Christian religion prevailed, till it was "supported and encouraged, as you tell us, by the laws of the empire": for I think, you will not say, or, if you should, you could not expect to be believed, that all, or the greatest part of those, that embraced the Christian religion, before it was supported by the laws of the empire, which was not 'till the fourth century, had actually miracles done before them, to work upon them. And all those, who were not eye-witnesses of miracles, done in their presence, 'tis plain, had no other miracles, than we have, that is upon report; and 'tis probable, not so many, nor so well attested, as we have. The greatest part then, of those, who were converted, at least in some of those ages, before Christianity was supported by the laws of the empire, I think you must allow, were wrought upon, by bare preaching, and such miracles as we still have, miracles at a distance, related miracles. In others, and those the greater number, prejudice was not so removed, that they were prevailed on to consider as they ought, i.e. in your language, to consider so as to embrace. If they had not so considered, in our days what, according to your scheme, must have been done to them, that did not consider, as they ought? Force must have been applied to them. What therefore, in the primitive church was to be done to them? Why! your succedaneum, miracles, actual miracles, such as you deny the Christian religion to be still accompanied with, and have been done in their presence, to work upon them. Will you say this was so, and make a new church-history for us, and out-do those writers, who have been thought pretty liberal of miracles? If you do not, you must confess, miracles supplied not the place of force, and so let fall all your fine contrivance about the necessity, either of force or miracles; and, perhaps you will think it, at last, a more becoming modesty, not to set the divine power and providence on work, by rules, and for the ends of your hypothesis, without having any thing in authentic history, much less in divine and unerring revelation to justify you. But force and power deserve something more than ordinary and allowable arts or arguments, to get and keep them: "Si violandum sit jus, regnandi causa violandum est."

If the testimony of miracles having been done, were sufficient to make the gospel prevail, without force, on those, who were not eye-witnesses of them, we have that still, and so, upon that account, need not force, to supply the want of it: but, if truth must have either the law of the country, or actual miracles to support it, what became of it, after the reign of Constantine the great, under all those emperors, that were erroneous or heretical? It supported itself in Piedmont, and France, and Turkey, many ages, without force or miracles: and it spread itself, in divers nations and kingdoms of the north and east, without any force, or other miracles than those, that were done many ages before. So that I think you will, upon second thoughts, not deny, but that the true religion is able to prevail now, as it did at first, and has done since, in many places, without assistance from the powers in being, by its own beauty, force and reasonableness, whereof well-attested miracles is a part.

★   ★   ★   ★   ★

The other reason, you seem to build on, is this, that when Christianity was received for the religion of the empire, miracles ceased; because there was then no longer any need of them; which I take to be the argument insinuated in these words, "Considering that those extraordinary means were not withdrawn, 'till, by their help, Christianity had prevailed to be received for the religion of the empire". If then, you can make it appear that miracles lasted 'till Christianity was received for the religion of the empire, without any other reason for their continuation, but to supply the want of the magistrate's assistance; and that they ceased, as soon as the magistrates became Christians; your argument will have some kind of probability, that, within the Roman empire, this was the method God used, for the propagating the Christian religion. But it will not serve to make good your position, "that the Christian religion cannot subsist and prevail by its own strength and light, without the assistance of miracles, or authority", unless you can shew, that God made use of miracles, to introduce and support it, in other parts of the world, not subject to the

Roman empire, 'till the magistrates there also became Christians. For the corruption of nature being the same without, as within the bounds of the Roman empire; miracles, upon your hypothesis, were as necessary to supply the want of the magistrate's assistance, in other countries, as in the Roman empire. For, I do not think, you will find the civil sovereigns were the first converted, in all those countries, where the Christian religion was planted after Constantine's reign; and, in all those, it will be necessary for you to shew us the assistance of miracles.

But let us see, how much your hypothesis is favoured by church-history. If the writings of the fathers of greatest name and credit are to be believed, miracles were not withdrawn, when "Christianity had prevailed to be received for the religion of the empire". Athanasius, the great defender of the catholic orthodoxy, writ the life of his contemporary, St. Anthony, full of miracles; which though some have questioned, yet the learned Dodwell allows to be writ by Athanasius: and the style evinces it to be his, which is also confirmed by other ecclesiastical writers.

★   ★   ★   ★   ★

These may suffice to shew, that, if the fathers of the Church, of greatest name and authority, are to be believed, miracles were not withdrawn, but continued down to the latter end of the fourth century, long after "Christianity had prevailed to be received for the religion of the empire".

But, if these testimonies of Athanasius, Chrysostom, Palladius, Ruffin, St. Hierom, and St. Austin, will not serve your turn, you may find much more to this purpose, in the same authors; and, if you please, you may consult also St. Basil, Gregory Nazianzen, Gregory Nyssen, St. Ambrose, St. Hilary, Theodoret, and others.

This being so, you must either deny the authority of these fathers, or grant that miracles continued in the Church, after "Christianity was received for the religion of the empire"; and then, they could not be, "to supply the want of the magistrate's assistance", unless they were to supply the want of what was not wanting; and therefore, they were continued for some other end. Which end of the continuation of miracles, when you are so far instructed in, as to be able to assure us, that it was different from that, for which God made use of them, in the 2nd and 3rd centuries: when you are so far admitted into the secrets of divine providence, as to be able to convince the world, that the miracles, between the apostles and Constantine's time, or any other period, you shall pitch on, were to supply the want of the magistrate's assistance, and those after, for some other purpose; what you say, may deserve to be considered. 'Till you do this, you will only shew the liberty you take, to assert, with great confidence, though without any ground, whatever will suit your system; and that you do not stick to make bold with the counsels of infinite wisdom, to make them subservient to your hypothesis.

And so I leave you to dispose of the credit of ecclesiastical writers, as you shall think fit; and, by your authority, to establish, or invalidate theirs, as you please. But this, I think, is evident, that he who will build his faith, or reasonings, upon miracles, delivered by church-historians, will find cause to go no farther than the apostles' time, or else not to stop at Constantine's: since the writers, after that period, whose word we readily take, as unquestionable in other things, speak of miracles in their time with no less assurance, than the fathers before the 4th century; and a great part of the miracles of the 2nd and 3rd centuries stand upon the credit of the writers of the 4th. So that that sort of argument, which takes and rejects the testimony of the ancients, at pleasure, as may best suit with it, will not have much force with those, who are not disposed to embrace the hypothesis, without any arguments at all.

You grant, "that the true religion has always light and strength of its own, i.e. without the assistance of force, or miracles, sufficient to prevail with all, that consider it seriously, and without prejudice: that, therefore, for which the assistance of force is wanting, is to make men consider seriously, and without prejudice." Now, whether the miracles, that we have still, miracles, done by Christ and his apostles, attested, as they are, by undeniable history, be not fitter to deal with men's prejudices, than force, and than force, which requires nothing, but outward conformity, I leave the world to judge. All the assistance, the true religion needs from authority, is only a liberty for it, to be truly taught; but it has seldom had that from the powers in being, in its first entry into their dominions, since the withdrawing of miracles: and yet I desire you to tell me, into what country the gospel, accompanied (as now it is) only with past miracles, has been brought by the preaching of men, who have laboured in it after the example of the apostles, where it did not so prevail over men's prejudices, "that as many as were ordained to eternal life", considered and believed it. Which, as you may see, Acts xiii. 48, was all the advance it made, even, when assisted with the gift of miracles: for neither then were all, or the majority, wrought on to consider, and embrace it.

But yet the gospel "cannot prevail, by its own light and strength"; and therefore miracles were to supply the place of force. How was force used? A law being made, there was a continued application of punishment to all those, whom it brought not to embrace the doctrine proposed. Were miracles so used, 'till force took place? For this, we shall want more new church-history, and, I think, contrary to what we read, in that part of it, which is unquestionable; I mean in the Acts of the apostles, where we shall find, that the then promulgators of the gospel, when they had preached, and done what miracles the Spirit of God directed, if they prevailed not, they often left them: "Then Paul and Barnabas waxed bold, and said, It was necessary that the word of God should first have been spoken to you: but seeing you put it from you, and judge yourselves unworthy—we turn to the Gentiles." "They shook off the dust of their feet against them, and came unto Iconium." "But when divers were hardened, and believed not, but spake evil of that way, before the multitude, he departed from them, and separated the disciples." "Paul was pressed in spirit, and testified to the Jews, that Jesus was Christ; and when they opposed themselves, and blasphemed, he shook his raiment, and said unto them your blood be upon your own heads, I am clean, from henceforth I will go unto the Gentiles." Did the Christian magistrate ever do so, who thought it necessary to support the Christian religion, by laws? Did they ever, when they had a while punished those, whom persuasions and preaching had not prevailed on, give off, and leave them to themselves, and make trial of their punishment upon others? Or, is this your way of force and punishment? If it be not, yours is not what miracles came to supply the room of, and so is not necessary. For you tell us, they are punished to make them consider, and they can never be supposed to consider, "as they ought, while they persist in rejecting"; and therefore, they are justly punished to make them so consider: so that not so considering, being the fault, for which they are punished, and the amendment of that fault, the end, which is designed to be attained, by punishing, the punishment must continue. But men were not always beat upon with miracles. To this perhaps, you will reply, that the seeing of a miracle, or two, or half a dozen, was sufficient to procure a hearing; but that being punished, once or twice, or half a dozen times, is not; for you tell us, "the power of miracles, communicated to the apostles, served altogether, as well as punishment, to procure them a hearing": where, if you mean, by hearing, only attention, who doubts but punishment may, also, procure that? If you mean, by hearing, receiving, and embracing, what is proposed, that even miracles themselves did not effect, upon all eye-witnesses. Why then, I beseech you, if one be to supply the place of the other, is one to be continued on those, who do reject, when the other was never long continued, nor, as I think we may safely say, often repeated, to those who persisted in their former persuasions?

After all, therefore, may not one justly doubt, whether miracles supplied the place of punishment; nay, whether you yourself, if you be true to your own principles, can think so? You tell us, that not to join "themselves to the true church, where sufficient evidence is offered, to convince men, that it is so is a fault, that it cannot be unjust to punish". Let me ask you, now: Did the apostles, by their preaching and miracles offer sufficient evidence to convince men that the Church of Christ was the true Church; or, which is, in this case, the same thing, that the doctrine, they preached was the true religion? If they did, were not those, who persisted in unbelief, guilty of a fault? And, if some of the miracles, done in those days, should now be repeated, and yet men should not embrace the doctrine, or join themselves to the Church, which those miracles accompanied, would you not think them guilty of a fault which the magistrate might justly, nay, ought to punish? if you would answer truly and sincerely to this question, I doubt you would think your beloved punishments necessary, notwithstanding miracles, "there being no other human means left". I do not make this judgment of you, from any ill opinion I have, of your good nature, but it is consonant to your principles: for, if not professing the true religion, where sufficient evidence is offered, by bare preaching, be a fault, and a fault justly to be punished by the magistrate, you will certainly think it much more his duty to punish a greater fault, as you must allow it is, to reject truth proposed with arguments and miracles, than with bare arguments: since you tell us, that the magistrate is "obliged to procure, as much as in him lies, that every man take care of his own soul, i.e. consider as he ought; which no man can be supposed to do, whilst he persists in rejecting": as you tell us, page 24.

Miracles, say you, supplied the want of force, " 'till, by their help, Christianity had prevailed to be received for the religion of the empire". Not that the magistrates had not as much commission then, from the law of nature, to use force, for promoting the true religion, as since: but, because the magistrates then, not being of the true religion, did not afford it the assistance of their political power. If this be so, and there be a necessity, either of force, or miracles, will there not be the same reason for miracles, ever since, even to this day, and so on, to the end of the world, in all those countries, where the magistrate is not of the true religion? Unless (as you urge it) you will say (what, without impiety, cannot be said) "that the wise and benign disposer of all things, has not furnished mankind, with competent means, for the promoting his own honour in the world, and the good of souls."

But to put an end to your pretence to miracles, as supplying the place of force. Let me ask you, whether, since the withdrawing of miracles, your moderate degree of force has been made use of, for the support of the Christian religion? If not, then miracles were not made use of, to supply the want of force, unless it were for the supply of such force, as Christianity never had, which is for the supply of just no force at all; or else, for the supply of the severities, which have been in use amongst Christians, which is worse than none at all. Force, you say, is necessary: what force? "Not fire and sword, not loss of estates, not maiming with corporal punishments, not starving and tormenting in noisome prisons": those you condemn. "Not compulsion: these severities" you say, "are apter to hinder, than promote the true religion, but moderate, lower penalties, tolerable inconveniences, such as should a little disturb and disease men." This assistance not being to be had from the magistrate in the first ages of Christianity, miracles, say you, were continued 'till "Christianity became the religion of the empire, not so much for any necessity there was, of them, all that while, for the evincing the truth of the Christian religion, as to supply the want of the magistrate's assistance. For the true religion, not being able to support itself, by its own light, and strength, without the assistance either of miracles, or of authority", there was a necessity of the one or the other; and therefore, whilst the powers, in being, assisted not, with necessary force, miracles supplied that want. Miracles, then, being to supply necessary force, and necessary force being only "lower, moderate penalties, some inconveniences, such as only disturb and disease a little": if you cannot shew that, in all countries, where the magistrates have been Christian, they have assisted with such force, 'tis plain that miracles supplied not the want of necessary force; unless, to supply the want of your necessary force, for a time, were to supply the want of an assistance, which true religion had not, upon the withdrawing of miracles, and I think, I may say, was never thought on, by any authority, in any age, or country, 'till you, now, above 1300 years after, made this happy discovery. Nay, Sir, since the true religion, as you tell us, cannot prevail, or subsist, without miracles, or authority, i.e. your moderate force; it must necessarily follow, that the Christian religion has, in all ages and countries, been accompanied, either with actual miracles, or such force: which, whether it be so or no, I leave you, and all sober men, to consider. When you can shew, that it has been so, we shall have reason to be satisfied with your bold assertion: That the Christian religion, as delivered in the New Testament, cannot "prevail, by its own light and strength, without the assistance" of your moderate penalties, or of actual miracles, accompanying it. But if ever since the withdrawing of miracles, in all Christian churches, where force has been thought necessary by the magistrate, to support the national, or (as, everywhere, it is called) the true religion, those severities have been made use of, which you (for a good reason) "condemn, as apter to hinder, than promote the true religion"; 'tis plain, that miracles supplied the want of such an assistance from the magistrate, as was apter to hinder, than promote, the true religion. And your substituting of miracles, to supply the want of moderate force, will shew nothing, for your cause, but the zeal of a man so fond of force, that he will, without any warrant from Scripture, enter into the counsels of the Almighty; and, without authority from history, talk of miracles, and political administrations, as may best suit his system.

3. SUMMARY OF LOCKE'S ARGUMENT

Locke's argument in brief is:

(a) That the "force" and compelling power of miracles never needs to be replaced by any equivalent, for it is something which the historical record transmits as well as the original events themselves.[1] The point of a miracle story is not just to record some remarkable event in the past; it must communicate that same power which belonged to the original situation.

(b) That his opponent is wrong on a point of fact when he argues that miracles ceased once the Christian religion was recognized by the State. There are no empirical grounds for believing that the civil power became an immediate substitute for the power of miracles.

(c) That if there were any parallel between the power of a miracle and civil power, since the civil power must persevere until the law is recognized and kept, miracles would have to be repeated until the Christian faith was universally accepted.

So the supposed equivalence of the power of miracle, and the power of the State is unfounded, and Locke is able to claim that what is distinctive about miracle is the power of God it displays. The apostles did "what miracles the spirit of God directed".

[1] And all this, despite the fact which Locke recognises (*Essay*, Bk. IV, Ch. 16, paras. 10, 11, and Ch. 18, para. 4), that a historic record will never give us anything like the clear and certain perceptual knowledge we would have had of the original occurrence had we witnessed it; which again suggests that a miraculous situation is significantly "more" than the ideas of sensation it contains. Incidentally, when in the *Essay*, Bk. IV. Ch. 18, para. 4, Locke seems to suggest that we can never be as sure that an alleged revelation came from God as that ideas agree or disagree, he must presumably mean in the absence of miraculous support, or else we must suppose a change in his views between the *Essay* (1690) and his *Third Letter* (1692) and the *Discourse* (1702).

INDEX

(i) GENERAL

Italics refer to *paragraphs* in *The Reasonableness of Christianity;* other references are to page numbers.

(ii) SCRIPTURE REFERENCES

The references are to paragraphs in *The Reasonableness of Christianity* and to pages elsewhere. In a very few cases the reference itself is not cited by Locke or otherwise made explicit.

The Reasonableness of Christianity

A Discourse of Miracles

A Third Letter Concerning Toleration
Chapter X